THE ATLANTIC CRITICAL STUDIES

WILLIAM SHAKESPEARE'S
Julius Caesar

RATRI RAY

ATLANTIC
PUBLISHERS & DISTRIBUTORS (P) LTD

Published by

ATLANTIC

PUBLISHERS & DISTRIBUTORS (P) LTD

7/22, Ansari Road, Darya Ganj,
New Delhi-110002
Phones : +91-11-40775252, 23273880, 23275880, 23280451
Fax : +91-11-23285873
Web : www.atlanticbooks.com
E-mail : orders@atlanticbooks.com

Branch Office
5, Nallathambi Street, Wallajah Road,
Chennai-600002
Phones : +91-44-64611085, 32413319
E-mail : chennai@atlanticbooks.com

Printed in India at Nice Printing Press, A-33/3A, Site-IV, Industrial Area, Sahibabad, Ghaziabad, U.P.

General Preface

The Atlantic Critical Studies are study-aids modeled on the study-aids available in England and America, among other places, and are primarily meant for the students of English literature in Indian universities.

However, in consideration of the local conditions and the various constraints under which our students have to study—non-availability of relevant critical books, dearth of foreign and Indian journals, inaccessibility to good, well-equipped libraries, just to mention a few of them—the models have been considerably improved upon, both qualitatively and quantitatively.

Thus, while these Studies are meant to be comprehensive and self-sufficient, the distinguished scholars who have prepared these study materials, have taken special care to combine lucidity and profundity in their treatment of the texts.

The select bibliography at the end is meant not only to acknowledge the sources used but also to help a student in the pursuit of further studies if he/she wants to.

Atlantic believes in quality and excellence. These studies will only reconfirm it.

MOHIT K. RAY

Chief Editor [English Literature]

Atlantic Publishers & Distributors (P) Ltd.,

New Delhi

Introduction

Many indeed were the poets and dramatists who wrote during the later part of the sixteenth and the early decades of the seventeenth centuries, but none of them speaks so intimately and immediately to us as Shakespeare does. He is the brightest star in that awe-inspiring galaxy of poets, dramatists and lyricists. He had the magic touch that turned everything he took up into gold. Not only did he experiment with many literary forms, but also developed them to the highest peak of excellence, whether it was drama, sonnets or lyrics.

This is one of the first points to strike one—his versatility. He tried his hand at many different kinds of plays and succeeded in each of them, whether tragedy, or comedy or history. There is no other dramatist of his time who can claim this. Marlowe wrote only tragedies and Ben Jonson, though he excelled at satirical comedies, did not succeed in anything else, and these were the only poets who could have rivalled Shakespeare. Since the work to be studied is a tragedy, it can be pointed out here that within the genre of tragedy itself, he had covered all the four main types prevalent in his day—Conqueror tragedy (*Macbeth*), Revenge tragedy (*Hamlet*), Domestic tragedy (*Romeo and Juliet*), and Villain tragedy (*Othello*). The present work *Julius Caesar*, is outside these four popular categories. These labels, it should be remembered, convey nothing of the richness and complexity with which he invested a popular form and uplifted it beyond all categories. When we take up the category of History play, the variety is astounding, though it would seem to be a genre comparatively limited in range. He wrote about English as well as Roman history and here also, the plays are not mere chronicles but can be classified differently. *Henry V* has been called a melodrama of triumph and *Julius Caesar* a tragedy.

What is surprising is that in each case, his material came from already existing sources, like narrative poems, stories, plays, etc. These were all inferior works, remembered by scholars today mainly because Shakespeare had used them. He used material from many different works for a single play and reorganised them to create a time-defying, unified whole.

Julius Caesar belongs to the group of the Roman plays. It is both a history play and a tragedy. There are three plays within this group, *Julius Caesar*, *Antony and Cleopatra* and *Coriolanus*. There are other plays concerned with Roman historical figures, but they do not fall within this group. *Titus Andronicus* is a Senecan tragedy and *Timon of Athens* a Problem comedy. *Julius Caesar* is a play faithful to history, for he had followed the Roman historian Plutarch very closely, yet it is not just a history play, as shall be seen in the chapter dealing with the genre of the play. It has been called, in addition to a historical tragedy, a morality play and a revenge tragedy. The complexity of the play can be imagined from these simple indications.

Indeed, as the ensuing study will show, every aspect of the play has intrigued scholars and critics. Everyone, whatever his or her attitude, agrees about one thing—Shakespeare's greatness as a dramatist. Shaw, though he did not approve of many of the plays, *Julius Caesar* in particular, still praised him:

> As far as sonority, imagery, wit, humour, energy of imagination, power over language, and whimsically keen eye for idiosyncrasies can make a dramatist, Shakespeare was the king of dramatists.[1]

NOTE

1. Shaw, The *Saturday Review*, 29 Jan., 1898, in Peter Ure (ed.), *Julius Caesar: A Casebook*, London: Macmillan, 1969, p. 40.

Contents

1

The Background

(a) The Socio-political Background

No writer stands independent of his time and milieu. The social structure, the political atmosphere, the religious and cultural tradition—everything influences him and his work. Shakespeare, too, was no exception. The authoritative social historian G.M. Trevelyan asserts:

> His works could never have been produced in any other period than those late Elizabethan and early Jacobean periods in which it was his luck to live. He could not have written as he did if the men and women among whom his days were passed had been other than they were.[1]

The socio-political background of any author, thus, bears an integral relationship to his work. We should therefore have a working knowledge of Shakespeare's background. A brief chronological time-table of the main events from Queen Elizabeth's succession to the death of our poet is given below. It contains, in brief, the chief political, social and religious events of the time. The last of these three is important because religion was an important issue of the time and influenced people's lives. Some events on the continent have also been mentioned.

A chronological table

1558 – Queen Mary I dies. Elizabeth I succeeds.

– Mary Queen of the Scots marries the French Dauphin.

’59 – Mary Queen of Scots declares herself the Queen of England, in spite of Queen Elizabeth.
– War between Spain and France ends.
– The Church of England re-established more firmly.

’60 – The Scottish Parliament establishes the Reformed Church and breaks with Rome and the Pope.

’61 – Mary Queen of Scots returns from France.
– She clashes with the Calvinists.

’62 – The Huguenots start emigrating from France to England.

’63 – Bubonic plague in Europe.

’64 – Shakespeare born. Galileo born.
– England is at war with Spain.
– The Thirty-Nine Articles adopted by the Church of England. Queen Elizabeth makes a laudable attempt to enforce uniformity of religion.

’67 – Mary Queen of Scots abdicates.
– Rugby Chapel founded.

’68 – Mary Queen of Scots flees to England and is held captive by Queen Elizabeth.

’69 – Rebellion of the Roman Catholic earls crushed.

’70 – Pope Pius V excommunicates Queen Elizabeth.

’74 – Burbage gets licence for the first theatre in London.

’76 – Tycho Brahe begins his astronomical observations.
– Burbage opens the first theatre in London.

’77 – Treaty with the Dutch signed.
– Sir Francis Drake begins his circumnavigation of the world.

’80 – Sir Francis Drake completes circumnavigation.

’81 – Conversion to Catholicism declared to be treason.
– Galileo discovers the Law of the Pendulum.

’83 – Plot against the Queen’s life discovered and scotched.

– Humphrey Gilbert takes possession of Newfoundland in the name of the Queen.

'84 – Sir Walter Raleigh discovers Virginia and names after the Queen. He arranges for colonization.

'86 – England wins the battle of Zutphen. Sir Philip Sidney dies in this battle.

– Plot against the Queen in which Mary Queen of Scots is implicated, and convicted of treason.

'87 – Rose Theatre built by Henslowe.

'88 – Defeat of the Spanish Armada by Sir Francis Drake.

'89 – Galileo publishes the result of his experiments with falling bodies.

'92 – John Davis discovers the Falkland islands.

'93 – Absence from the Church on Sundays made punishable by law.

'95 – Robert Southwell the mystical poet executed for celebrating Mass.

'96 – England, France and Netherlands form alliance against Spain.

'97 – Irish Rebellion. Statutory provision for Poor Relief. Beggary made illegal.

'98 – The Bodleian Library begun. The Globe Theatre opened.

1603 – Queen Elizabeth dies. Accession of King James I.

'04 – Peace with Spain. Acts against priests and recusants. Anglican canons made.

'05 – Repression of Puritans and Catholics. Gunpowder plot.

'08 – Failure for the King in his plans for union with Scotland.

'10 – Judicial decision against royal proclamations.

'11 – The Parliament is dissolved.

'12 – Alliance with German Protestant princes.

– Witches hanged at Lancashire.

1616 – Shakespeare dies.

Though this table is very sketchy, yet a careful study of it will reveal the main features of the contemporary socio-political situation. When Shakespeare was born, the throne of England was in a very unstable condition. There were plots against the Queen by her own subjects, while abroad there was constant warfare with the neighbouring nations. Quite a few years passed before the Queen could feel comparative security on the throne and turn her attention to bringing political stability to England in her relationships with her immediate neighbours. The policies that the Queen adopted, both at home and abroad, were wise and tolerant and she brought peace and stability to her country. Under her benevolent governance, even the vexatious and bloody controversies over religion came to an end. Perhaps the most signal achievement of her reign was the establishing of a definite and uniform religious discipline in England. G.M. Trevelyan points out:

> In the year in which the Queen succeeded her sister Mary, Puritanism was mainly a foreign doctrine imported from Geneva and Rhineland; when she died it was rootedly and characteristically English.[2]

Today, the Elizabethan Age is known as an age of peace, prosperity and expansion in every field. As far as the social framework is concerned, class barriers did exist, but it was an accepted feature, not resented by anyone. This was because the feudal lords rarely oppressed any of those who were in their power. It was a healthy society as described by G.M. Trevelyan:

> English society was based not on equality but freedom—freedom of opportunity and freedom of personal intercourse. Such was the Engand known and approved by Shakespeare.[3]

Each member of this society had self-reliance and self-respect, for he earned a fair wage for honest labour. No bondmen or slaves existed.

Industry and trade also prospered. The factory system had come into existence. The capitalist employer provided jobs to a great number of men as he was anxious to keep his factory working at full capacity. Mining expanded to a very great extent so that metals like lead, copper, iron and tin became available to all.

National pride climbed a high peak as a result of the two remarkable achievements of Sir Francis Drake—the defeat of the hitherto invincible Spanish Armada and the circumnavigation of the world. The sense of joy and exuberance which pervaded England is reflected in the literature of the time:

> By the end of Elizabeth's reign, not only was England commercially and financially reviving and expanding on a modern basis but her ancient rivals were in rapid decline.[4]

(b) The Literary Background

Not for nothing is the Elizabethan Age known as the Golden Age of England. As such, Elizabethan England invites comparison with Periclean Greece and Augustan Rome. As has been explained in the foregoing section, the age was a prosperous one from the social point of view and it was even more so as far as literature was concerned. A chronological table is given below which covers the main literary events of the time. It begins with the first performance of *Ralph Roister Doister* which took place ten years before Shakespeare's birth. His own plays are not mentioned here as they will be given later. (*Vide* Chapter 2, "Life and Works" infra)

A chronological table

1554	–	Sir Philip Sidney and Lyly born.
	–	*Ralph Roister Doister* performed.
'57	–	Tottel's *Miscellany*. Lord North's *The Dial of Princes*.
'58	–	Kyd, Greene, Peele, Lodge born.
'61	–	Bacon born. *Gorboduc* performed.
'63	–	Drayton and Donne born.
'64	–	Shakespeare born. Marlowe born.
'66	–	*Supposes* by Gascoigne. Painter's *Palace of Pleasure*.

- '67 – Campion and Nashe born. Pickering's *Interlude of Vice*.
- '75 – Heywood and Tourneur born. *Appius and Virginia*, *Gammer Gurton's Needle*.
- '76 – *Paradyse of Daynty Devises*.
- '77 – Holinshed's *Chronicles*. Grange's *Golden Aphroditis*.
- '78 – Lyly's *Euphues*.
- '79 – Spenser's *Shepheardes Calender*. Gosson's *Schole of Abuse*.
- '82 – Hakluyt's *Voyages*.
- '85 – Kyd's *The Spanish Tragedy*.
- '86 – Sir Philip Sidney dies. Lyly's *Endimion*.
- '87 – Marlowe's *Tamburlaine*, Lyly's *Gallathea*.
- '89 – Marlowe's *Jew of Malta*. Puttenham's *Arte of English Poesie*.
- '90 – *Faerie Queene* Bks I-III, Sidney's *Arcadia*.
- '91 – *Astrophel and Stella*, Marlowe's *Edward II*.
- '92 – Daniel's *To Delia*, Marlowe's *Hero and Leander*.
- '95 – Spenser's *Amoretti* and *Epithalamion*. Sidney's *Apology for Poetry*.
- '99 – Spenser dies. Ben Jonson's *Every Man Out of His Humour*.
- '1600 – *England's Helicon*. Ben Jonson's *Cynthia's Revels*.
- '01 – Dekker and Marston's *Satiromastix*. Jonson's *Poetaster*.
- '03 – Dowland's *Third Book of Songs*, *Sejanus*.
- '04 – Chapman's *Bussy D'Ambois*, Marston's *Malcontent*.
- '05 – Drayton's *Collected Poems*.
- '06 – Lyly dies. *Yorkshire Tragedy*, *Volpone*, *Revenger's Tragedy*.
- '07 – Beaumont and Fletcher's *Knight of the Burning Pestle*.

’09 – *Philaster*, Fulke Greville’s *Mustapha.*

’10 – Ben Jonson’s *The Alchemist.*

’11 – *The Authorized Version of The Bible.*

’12 – Chapman’s *Iliad*, Webster’s *The White Devil.*

’13 – Overbury and Constable die. *Purchas His Pilgrimage.*

’14 – Overbury’s *Characters*, Lodge’s *Works of Seneca*, Raleigh’s *History of the World*, Jonson’s *Bartholomew Fair*, Webster’s *Duchess of Malfi.*

’16 – Shakespeare dies. Chapman’s *The Whole Works of Homer*, Jonson’s *Works*, his *Devil is an Ass.*

(This table mentions only a few of the works written and published during this time.)

As can be seen from this table, the years covering Shakespeare’s birth in 1564 to his death in 1616 were the most productive ones. During Sidney’s lifetime, the most notable works had not yet come into existence and so, his *Apologie for Poetry* decries English drama. The state of English literature, however, improved by leaps and bounds, the drama most of all. During our poet’s childhood many plays were already being written and staged, all of an inferior kind. Only *Gorboduc* is praised by Sidney:

> ...as it is full of stately speeches and well-sounding phrases, climbing to the heights of Seneca’s style and as full of notable morality which it doth most delightfully teach, and so obtain the very end of poesy.[5]

In 1587, a play was performed by a group of eight authors (among whom was included Lord Bacon), for the Queen’s entertainment. Entitled, *The Misfortunes of King Arthur*, today this play has only historical value. This was the childhood of Elizabethan drama, to be soon outcared by Marlowe, Shakespeare and all the others.

Shakespeare had pre-existing models to follow, and occasionally improve upon, not only in drama but in sonnets, songs and narrative poems as well. In this respect also the early Elizabethan Age presents a prospect marginally better than the prospect of drama. Spenser's *Shepheardes Calender* and the first few books of *Faerie Queene* had been published before our poet wrote his *Venus and Adonis*, his first narrative poem. The sonnets of Wyatt and Surrey had been published by Tottel in his *Miscellany*. It was only in the last decade of the century that the famous sonnet-sequences were written. From 1680 onwards, the countless love-songs started to be written, and were published under attractive names: *Paradyse of Daynty Devises, England's Helicon* are but two of them. The poets are mostly anonymous and go under the name of "the Elizabethan nest of singing-birds". After giving a list of the features of these lyrics Yvor Winters says:

> The best poems in the early school are among the most perfect examples of the classical virtues to be found in English poetry.[6]

The Elizabethan Age, as it progressed, brought forth a scintillating wealth of many kinds of poems: narrative, lyrical, discursive, religious, etc. Prose, too, flourished in the hands of writers like Lord Bacon, Sir Thomas Browne, Burton, Hooker and others.

In the present instance, drama is of great interest. Here, in tragedy, the prevailing influence was that of Seneca. Kyd's famous *The Spanish Tragedy*, which became the prototype for all revenge tragedies, was in the Senecan mode. Another such popular tragedy was *Tamburlaine* by Marlowe. This was so successful that Marlowe had to produce a sequel and both bear the imprint of his artistic talent. Burbage and later Henslowe established theatre halls where plays came to be regularly performed and became one of the chief sources of entertainment for the Elizabethan public. The great dramatists experimented with different kinds of plays and honed their skills to perfection. Tragedies of four different kinds, comedies catering to three distinct classes, chronicle plays and farces were poured forth in an endless stream. Besides Shakespeare, the late Elizabethan Age produced the works of many others, though drama reached its highest peak towards the end of the Elizabethan age, and the beginning of the Jacobean. Ben Jonson, Webster, Chapman, Tourneur, Middleton, Marston,

Dekker, Heywood—these are the names of some of the most popular dramatists.

The tragedies of this time have been designated as the Blood-and-thunder tragedies and divided into four categories. Conqueror tragedies centred around an overwhelmingly ambitious person, like the tragedies of Marlowe. The Revenge tragedy was started by Kyd and started proliferating immediately after. Villain tragedy was the third kind, *The Changeling* of Middleton and Rowley being a very fine example. Our poet's *Othello* is often categorised as one. The fourth kind of tragedy was the domestic tragedy. The two anonymous plays, *The Yorkshire Tragedy* and *Arden of Feversham* are examples of this last kind.

Comedy is not very important in the present instance but it may be noted that different kinds of comedies flourished during the period. Shakespeare himself had written three kinds of comedies: the romantic, the problem comedies and the romances. He did not try his hand at the satirical city comedies in which Ben Jonson excelled. Tragi-comedies were being written by Beaumont and Fletcher. There was thus, great variety in tragedy as well as in comedy.

Another kind of play being written at this time was the chronicle play or the history play. This is a kind of play that cannot be labelled as a tragedy or a comedy but exists in its own right. Some of them, like Marlowe's *Edward II* ends in the death of the hero, causing it to be called a historical tragedy. This is the case with some of Shakespeare's own history plays as well, especially *Richard II*. Not many writers wrote successful chronicle plays. Shakespeare, with his splendid pageant of historical heroes, remained unrivalled in this field, no one equalled him.

Another form of popular entertainment was the masque. These were very popular and were specially suited for celebrating happy occasions like betrothals, marriages, etc. Mythical and supernatural characters like gods and goddesses, nymphs and satyrs were brought on the stage and this naturally involved the use of sumptuous costumes. Such productions were very expensive and were usually produced by the court and the aristocracy. In Queen Elizabeth's court, the noble lords and ladies themselves participated. Ben Jonson wrote many well-known masques. They are to be found incorporated within the framework of Shakespeare's plays also. The masque celebrating the betrothal of Ferdinand and Miranda in *The Tempest* is a well-known example of Shakespeare's use of the masque to enhance the beauty of his plays.

Apart from these, there were the farces, causing boisterous laughter. It was usually from the lower section of society that the characters for farces were taken. Shakespeare did not favour this form. It was only once that he wrote such a play. Queen Elizabeth had been charmed by Sir John Falstaff of Shakespeare's history play *King Henry IV*, Pt I and had specially commissioned a play showing "the fat knight in love". *The Merry Wives of Windsor* was the play our poet wrote to please his sovereign and it is usually taken to be a farce—the only such of Shakespeare.

The times in which Shakespeare wrote, thus, were times that showed the expansion and efflorescence of England in every respect. The form of drama reached a height of excellence rarely touched since then. As F.P. Wilson explains:

> The drama is at its greatest during those years between 1590 and 1620 when the actors were neither poverty-stricken vagabonds nor hangers-on at Court, and when the audience was most representative of City, Country and Court.[7]

NOTES

1. G.M. Trevelyan, *Illustrated English Social History*, Vol. 2. Harmondsworth: Penguin Books Ltd., p. 125.
2. *Ibid.*, p. 86.
3. *Ibid.*, p. 62.
4. *Ibid.*, p. 123.
5. Sir Philip Sidney, "An Apology for Poetry", in D.J. Enright and Chickera, eds., *English Critical Texts*. Oxford: Oxford University Press, Twenty-first Impr., 2002, p. 40.

6. Y. Winters, "The Sixteenth Century Lyric in England", in P.J. Alpers, ed., *Elizabethan Poetry*. Oxford: Oxford University Press, 1967, p. 96.
7. F.P. Wilson, "Elizabethan and Jacobean Drama", in R.J. Kaufmann, ed., *Elizabethan Drama*. Oxford: Oxford University Press, 1961, pp. 4-5.

2

Life and Works

(a) A Short Biography

Many of the great Elizabethan writers remain enigmatic figures since very little is known of their personal life. This is not quite the case with Shakespeare. There is a wealth of biographical material in his case, and one can be certain of many important dates and events. Irving Ribner, pointing out this feature, has also explained it:

> As a dramatist, Shakespeare acquired considerable reputation during his own lifetime. It continued to grow in the centuries following his death in 1616, accumulating as it did an accretion of legends and anecdotes.[1]

First of all, a chronological table of the important events of Shakespeare's life is given below.

A chronological table of Shakespeare's life

1564	–	Apr. 23, the supposed date of birth of Shakespeare.
	–	Apr. 26, Shakespeare is baptised at the Parish Church.
'71	–	Possible time of enrolment in the local Grammar School.
'78	–	His father suffers severe financial loss.
'82	–	Shakespeare is married to Anne Hathaway.
'83	–	Birth of Susannah, his first daughter.
'85	–	Baptism of the twins, Hamnet and Judith.

'86 – His supposed departure for London.
'93 – *Venus and Adonis* published by a fellow villager.
'94 – *Rape of Lucrece*, *Titus Andronicus*.
'96 – Tragic death of Hamnet his only son, at 12 years.
'97 – He buys New Place, the second largest property.
'99 – He buys shares in the Globe Theatre.
1602 – The birth of his first grandchild. He also buys one hundred and seven acres of land.
'04 – His company comes under royal patronage and is given the name of the King's Men.
'11 – He retires from the company and comes back to settle in his native village.
'13 – *The Tempest* staged.
'16 – Jan. 25—His Last Will and Testament drawn up.
– Apr. 23—He dies on his fifty-second birthday.
– Apr. 25—Buried in the Chancel of Stratford Church.

The exact date of his birth is not known, but the date of his christening had been recorded in the Register of Baptism in the Parish Church of Stratford-upon-Avon, in official Latin:

1564, Apr. 26, Gulielmus Filius Johannes Shakespeare.[2]

Usually a baby was christened three days after its birth, and so it is generally assumed that our poet was born on the twenty-third of April at Stratford-upon-Avon, in the county of Warwickshire. This was, according to the saints' calendar, the auspicious St. George's Day, who is the patron saint of England.

Though nothing is known about his infancy, it can be safely assumed that he had a normal, secure and happy childhood. He was the eldest son and as such he had a strong position in the family. His father, John Shakespeare, was a prosperous tradesman and his mother, Mary Arden, came from a family socially slightly higher than that of his father's. John Shakespeare was not only a prosperous trader, he was also a man of high integrity and this was valued by the village. He gradually rose higher and higher in the social scale and finally became the mayor of Stratford and the alderman in 1565. This was such a high position that he could claim the status of a gentleman. This meant the landed gentry as differentiated from a trader. Shakespeare came from such a family. This was of great importance in a feudal society.

The village in which he spent his infancy and youth was surrounded by unspoilt countryside. He retained vivid memories of this and reproduced it repeatedly in his works in wonderful verbal pictures. The foundations of the descriptions of nature were laid at this time in the mind of the child.

His father was a Justice of Peace and also the High Bailiff of his village. As such, he had to take active part in judicial matters. It is thought by the biographers that Shakespeare, as soon as he was old enough, accompanied him to the law courts and thus gained first-hand knowledge of legal procedures.

The establishment of Grammar Schools, which had been started by the Queen in the second half of the century had by this time, become part and parcel of life. Stratford also had its own Grammar School in which the classics were taught. It can hardly be said with assurance exactly when our poet entered this school. According to some, he was but seven and according to others, nine. He was, however, enrolled in this school where he acquired his store of knowledge. Ben Jonson's opinion that he had only "small Latin and less Greek" is well-known, but actually Shakespeare's knowledge of the classics was not contemptible by any means. He studied in this school for at least seven years. As to at what age he left the school, the biographers do not agree. Whatever he studied there was retained in his memory and repeatedly used in all his works, whether in the large scope of a history play, or in a small reference to classical myths.

There are reliable records of the workings of the schools of this age. Classes started at six in the morning in summer and at seven in winter, and continued till five in the evening. There were, however, frequent breaks during the day, which came up to a total of two and a half hours. The curriculum consisted mainly of Latin grammar and literature. The following works were prescribed:

Poetry : Mantuan's imitation of Virgil named the *Bucolica*, Virgil's own *Eclogues* and *The Aeneid*. Horace's Poems and Ovid's *Metamorphoses*.

Prose : Caesar, Livy and Cicero.

Drama : Seneca's tragedies, and the comedies of Plautus and Terence.

All these works were studied in their original Latin. A knowledge of the language therefore, was taken for granted. Irving Ribner comments on the surprising amount of classical literature imparted to the schoolboys:

> In the light of the training, a normal schoolboy would have undergone at the Stratford Grammar School, it is difficult to understand why the extent of Shakespeare's learning has been so much a subject for debate.[3]

There is, however, another opinion, totally different, about Shakespeare's schooling. John Dover Wilson holds that Shakespeare did not attend any of these schools, for they were all run by Protestants, whereas his family was a staunch Catholic. Dover Wilson is of the opinion that John Shakespeare would have put his son in the service of a Catholic nobleman. He would have, in such a case, got his education along with the sons of the house and also gained first-hand knowledge of the lifestyle of the aristocracy.

Knowledge from the schoolbooks was not the only knowledge that Shakespeare got at this time. He soaked up knowledge from other sources as well. One such source was the watching of the plays put up by travelling actors. The great noblemen of the time, specially the Earls of Leicester and of Warwickshire (Shakespeare's own county) patronised theatrical groups which put up plays all over the country. Many such groups visited his village and he must have seen many plays.

It is definitely known that he came across Anne Hathaway in his eighteenth year. She herself was fully twenty-six at the time, but she charmed him and they got married on Nov. 28, 1582. Their first daughter Susannah, was born next year, and the twins, Hamnet and Judith, two years later. Nothing is known of Shakespeare's married life. Hamnet died in 1596 at twelve years of age. No one was left to carry on the line.

By the time that Shakespeare was twenty-one, he was already a married man with a wife and no less than three children to support. It was necessary to find some means of livelihood and there are many stories of his activities at this time. It is said that he was holding a teacher's job at a school near his village, and it is also said that he was acting in a theatrical company. There is one anecdote which is generally accepted, though it may not be true. This story says that Shakespeare and a few other young men had poached in the preserves of Sir Thomas Lucy. Shakespeare was caught and put into prison. Perhaps he was whipped or threatened with whipping. It may be that this incident made him decide to leave the village and go to London in search of a livelihood.

It was probably in 1586 that he came to London. It is not known for sure how he spent his life for the next six years. These are known as the Dark years and there are many theories about them. Perhaps he held the horses of the noblemen who came to the theatre, perhaps he had managed to get a job of some kind in the theatre. It is known however, that he came into contact with one Richard Field, a young man from his own village. Field had become an established printer in London. It was he who published *Venus and Adonis* in 1593 and *The Rape of Lucrece* next year.

The chronological table of the literary background (Chapter 2, *supra*) shows that Shakespeare and Marlowe were born in the same year. They also reached London at very much the same time. The 1580s was a glorious decade for Elizabethan England. Pioneering work was being done in the field of the arts as well as in geography. *Astrophel and Stella*, the first sequence of love-sonnets, was being composed by Sir Philip Sidney and Spenser, in Ireland, was writing *The Faerie Queene*. London was the cultural centre of the country and young men of talent from all over England were converging there. Lyly, having achieved fame with his *Euphues*, had turned his attention to drama. Two of his comedies had been presented to the Queen. The University Wits, Thomas Kyd, Robert Greene and Thomas Nashe had all settled in London. Marlowe achieved instant fame by *Tamburlaine* in 1587. It was an exhilarating time, with new horizons opening out in all directions. F.E. Halliday describes the time:

> It was a proud, mercurial, quarrelsome vivid society, a mediaeval people magically vitalised by contact with the Renaissance, quivering with energy.[4]

Shakespeare quickly became part of this heady London life and started the slow climb to fame. It is paradoxical that the first mention of his name in London should be due to professional jealousy. It is given by Greene in a work which is remembered only for this reference—a spiteful one, to Shakespeare.

It is a pamphlet called *Greene's Groatsworth of Wit bought with a Million of Repentances*, and contains, at the end, a letter addressed to his friends Marlowe, Nashe and Peele. Greene cautions them against actors:

> Yes, trust them not: for there is an upstart crow, beautified with our feathers that with his Tyger's heart wrapt in a player's hyde, supposes he is as well able to bombast out a blank verse as the best of you; and being an absolute Johannes fac totum, is in his own conceit the only Shakescene in a country.[5]

This gives two clear references to Shakespeare. First of all there is the name Shake-scene and secondly the line "Tyger's heart wrapt in a Player's hyde" which is an adaptation of a line in Shakespeare's popular trilogy *Henry VI*, Part III: "O tiger's heart, wrapped in a woman's hide." This malicious backbiting serves to make us realise that Shakespeare was becoming well-known in the theatrical world—enough to cause alarm and jealousy in the well-established University Wits.

These early years are today known as his time of apprenticeship and were highly productive. The two myth-based narrative poems *Venus and Adonis* and *The Rape of*

Lucrece were written at this time as well as the sonnet-sequence dedicated to Mr W.H. *Henry VI* trilogy, *Richard III*, *Titus Andronicus*, *The Comedy of Errors*, *The Two Gentlemen of Verona* and *The Taming of the Shrew* were all written at this time. The plays were highly successful on the stage. *Titus Andronicus*, one of his least attractive plays was so popular that it came to be performed by the three best companies of the time, those patronised by the Earls of Derby, Pembroke and Sussex. As has been pointed out earlier (*Vide* Chapter 1, Introduction, *supra*), many playwrights were writing at this time, but all of them had a limited range. Kyd and Marlowe wrote highly popular tragedies and there their talents drew rein. Shakespeare was the only one who could give, even at this early stage, histories, tragedies and comedies with equal facility. By 1594 he had hardly anyone to equal him, whether in drama, poems or sonnets.

There were many theatrical groups in London at this time and the best of them was the one known as the Lord Chamberlaine's Men. Shakespeare became the writer of this group and thus held a position of great importance. Every group depended on its writer for its success and survival. Just as the writer needed the group. Shakespeare continued in this healthy symbiotic relationship with this group till his retirement.

Even before he was thirty, he had become a highly successful man. He came to Stratford and stayed there for four months. By this time his children were of an age to need schooling, and his father was an old man of sixty. It is thought that both *Venus and Adonis* and *Richard III* were written here.

It was at this time that one of the most important relationships of his life took root. He met Henry Wriothesley, the Earl of Southampton. This handsome aristocrat was nearly ten years younger than him, and an enthusiastic patron of arts. An intense relationship developed between Shakespeare and him, expressed in his sonnets. Both of the narrative poems are dedicated to him and Shakespeare professes, in the Dedication, a deep and enduring love for his patron. Different aspects of this relationship are expressed in the sonnets. The Earl's patronage gave Shakespeare, not only one of the most intense experiences of his life, but security. A.L. Rowse, pointing out the difference between him and the other poets in respect of social security, says:

> It meant all the difference between the dreadful insecurity poor Greene and others had died of, and having firm ground under his feet.[6]

This means that Shakespeare was financially secure then, with a prosperous artistic career to look forward to. He bought a share in his company which, besides making money from the public performances, also performed at Court, and this brought honour. London was being annually ravaged by the Plague and Shakespeare was the only dramatist to survive it. Kyd was already dead. Peele would die in a few years. Lyly and Lodge had discontinued writing for the stage and Nashe had drifted away to writing pamphlets. Marlowe would have been a worthy rival, but he was killed in a drunken brawl in a tavern. The only playwright with genius nearly equal to his own was Ben Jonson, but he had not started to write yet. Shakespeare, thus, was without a rival either on the stage or in life. It is true that in the sonnets he mentions a rival, but perhaps it was Marlowe, who died soon after.

His comedies offered exactly the kind of light-hearted entertainment that the audience wanted. The exuberant and musical comedies *Love's Labour Lost*, *A Midsummer Night's Dream* and *The Merchant of Venice* enthralled the audience. The university students had taken Shakespeare to their bosom. There are rapturous references to him in a poem by Henry Willoughby, an Oxford undergraduate who was clearly an admirer:

> Yet Tarquin plucked his glistering grape
> And Shakespeare paints poor Lucrece's rape.[7]

Fame and success was his, but tragedy was lurking very near. In 1597, he was at Stratford when his only son Hamnet died. The family line ended here.

Shakespeare was so prosperous by this time that he was able to buy New Place, which was the second best property in

Stratford. He could now claim the status of landed gentry. His father had applied to the Herald's College some years ago for a coat-of-arms. Shakespeare followed it up and the request was granted. So he came back to London as a member of the landed gentry.

There is a famous reference to him and his works in *Palladis Tamia* by Francis Meres, written in 1598. Meres compares him with classical Roman dramatists Plautus and Seneca in the fields of comedy and tragedy respectively:

> As Plautus and Seneca are accounted the best for Comedy and Tragedy among the Latines: Shakespeare among the English is the most excellent for both kinds.[8]

This work is of great value as it mentions the two narrative poems, "the sugred sonnets", and eleven of his plays, thus dating them firmly.

King James's accession to the throne was a great event, for he took Shakespeare's company under his wing. It became known as the King's Men, the highest honour in the land. Hereafter can be found many records of this time of his life, presenting the picture of a busy, popular and creative person.

The four great tragedies were written at this time. *Hamlet* was the last of the plays produced in the time of Elizabeth and *Othello* was performed in 1604 in King James's court, while 1606 saw the staging of *King Lear* and *Macbeth*. Along with the tragedies the Problem comedies and the Chronicle plays were also being written and performed. There is a notable change of tone in his works of this time. A sombre note has crept in, ousting exuberance:

> The Jacobean poetry is one of compression and lacks the definition of the Elizabethan; thought is packed tight and imagery reduced to the single word of metaphors.[9]

His first grandchild was born in 1608 and it was in this year that his mother passed away. Next year, in 1609, his sonnets which had been in circulation for about a decade in manuscript form, were now published. He started writing his last Romances. In 1611, he retired from his company and settled in his native village as a prosperous and respected man.

Retirement did not mean inaction, for he continued coming to London. His name occurs in many of the documents of this time. In 1612, there was a royal betrothal and *The Tempest* was staged on this occasion. It is thought that Shakespeare himself enacted the role of Prospero.

His time was running out now and in Jan. 1616, his will was drawn up. A few months later, on his birthday, the twenty-third of April, he breathed his last. This was his fifty-second birth anniversary. There is an elaborate tomb on his grave, with his coat-of-arms and many allegorical figures and inscriptions. The most well-known of these is an epitaph in the shape of a quatrain, thought to have been written by him:

Good friend, for Jesus sake forbeare,
To dig the dust enclosed here!
Blest be the man that spares the stones,
And curst be he that moves my bones.[10]

(b) Shakespeare's Works

It has not been always possible to get the exact date of each of his works. The dates of performances can be obtained with fair accuracy. Henslowe used to make entries in his *Diary* of the dates of the performances. The *Stationer's Register* also has entries. Basing the dates on these and other documents, modern scholars have divided his career into four phases as given below. The phases, however, should not be treated like water-tight compartments, for there are possible overlappings.

Phase I

1591 – *The Comedy of Errors.*

'92 – *The Two Gentlemen of Verona, Henry VI, Pts I, II, III.*

'93 – *Richard III, Romeo and Juliet, Venus and Adonis.*

Phase II

'94 – *The Rape of Lucrece, The Sonnets, Titus Andronicus, King Richard II, A Midsummer Night's Dream, Love's Labour's Lost, The Taming of the Shrew, King John.*

’95 – *The Merchant of Venice.*

’97 – *Henry IV, Part I.*

’98 – *Henry IV, Part II, The Merry Wives of Windsor.*

’98 – *King Henry V, Much Ado About Nothing, Julius Caesar.*

1600 – *As You Like It, Twelfth Night.*

Phase III

1602 – *Hamlet, Troilus and Cressida, All’s Well that Ends Well.*

’04 – *Measure for Measure, Othello.*

’05 – *King Lear.*

’06 – *Macbeth.*

’07 – *Antony and Cleopatra.*

’08 – *Coriolanus, Timon of Athens, Pericles.*

Phase IV

’10 – *Cymbeline, The Winter’s Tale, The Tempest.*

’11 – *Henry VIII.*

The different phases, as given above, melt into one other and have been designated according to his artistic development. The first one is that of Experiment and goes on till 1594. According to some critics, it can be extended to 1595 when *The Merchant of Venice* was written. During this period, our poet was engaged primarily in re-writing old plays. There are many traces of immaturity, especially in the style. Yet it cannot be denied that the poetry of this time is rich and exuberant. There is a considerable amount of ornamentation and play on words. The characters lack in depth.

Next comes the phase of development, which stretches from 1595 to 1601. He is enjoying the security and self-respect that the patronage of the Earl of Southampton has brought to him. The struggle for establishing himself is over and he can turn his attention to the perfecting of his art. He, having fully mastered the technique of dramatic blank verse, can now modulate it to the demands of each individual character. As a result the characters gradually become more realistic, giving evidence of deep psychological insight. The plots of the history plays as well as those of the golden comedies show how adept he has become at collecting material from many different sources and arranging and adapting them to his own advantage.

The prevailing mood of the third phase is a sombre and gloomy one. His attention is now focused on the frailties of human nature and the unavoidable presence of evil. This preoccupation is reflected not only in the tragedies but in the comedies also which, for this reason, are called the Dark Comedies as contrasted with the earlier group which is known as the Golden or the Happy Comedies.

But, being a man and an artist of extraordinary mental powers, Shakespeare triumphed over all this to emerge into the peace and tranquillity of the last phase. Here is the evidence of a fully mature wisdom that accepts the presence of evil along with goodness. The Romances he wrote during this time illustrate this wisdom.

(c) Notes on Individual Works

The Comedy of Errors

This is the shortest of his plays and is at present thought by the scholars to be his first. It is modelled on *Menaechmi*, a well-known comedy of Plautus. Even in this first play Shakespeare's stage sense is in evidence, for he has altered Plautus's plot. In the Plautine play, there is but one pair of twins but our poet has introduced two. The play is a hilarious comedy based on mistaken identities, and Shakespeare's play, having two pairs of twins, is naturally far more complicated. It is not known when it was performed first, but it was presented at Court in 1594. Critics agree that it might have been put up on the public stage before this.

The Two Gentlemen of Verona

Some scholars think that this is his first play. Whether that is right or not, this is definitely the first of his romantic comedies. The characters are balanced with each other, for there are two fathers, two servants and two pairs of lovers.

This makes for a well-balanced, symmetrical plot. There are two themes here—that of friendship and that of love. The stress falls on the former. Two themes of a highly serious nature, which will occupy him till the very end of his career, those of forgiveness and reconciliation, occur here for the first time. An important Shakespearean character, that of the Clown, occurs here.

Henry VI, Pts I, II and III

Here indeed, Shakespeare has no parallel in the creation of the patriotic and colourful pageants. These are not mere depiction of historical events, for he takes up the serious issues of kingship and its many responsibilities. The material for the history plays came from Holinshed's *Chronicles*. This trilogy was so popular that it was performed, in 1592, three times in eight days. Reaching its climax in regicide, the cycle presents a world of betrayal and conflict. Shakespeare was already becoming a threat to the University. Wits as can be seen in Greene's spiteful reference to one of the lines in this trilogy, "O tiger's heart wrapped in a woman's hide" (*Vide* the section on Life).

Richard III

This is more of a tragedy than a history play. The hero, King Richard III, is a Marlovian figure. This shows that Shakespeare is still under the influence of Marlowe, for the earlier Henry VI trilogy also had given evidence of Marlowe's influence in its poetry. In this play, it is the character that shows the influence. King Richard III however, is a far more complex figure than Marlowe's heroes. This shows that Shakespeare's psychological insight is already deeper than that of Marlowe and that his poetry is strong enough to portray this complexity. This is the second longest play of our poet, *Hamlet* being the longest.

Romeo and Juliet

The first of his romantic tragedies, this play tells the story of conflict between two families in which a pair of star-crossed lovers is caught. Here it is Fate, more than character, that dominates the action. "Character is destiny" is the maxim generally applied to Elizabethan tragedies, but it is not applicable in this case. Shakespeare took up an Italian story and followed it quite closely. The character of Mercutio is an original one, for there is no such character in the story that he followed. The pair of lovers has passed into common life as the very symbol of young lovers. Shakespeare's power of versification is already making itself felt, especially in the Queen Mab speech of Mercutio.

Venus and Adonis

Narrative poems based on Greek myths were very popular in those days. This poem became so highly appreciated that it ran through ten or eleven editions. It amply proves the versatility of his genius. It is composed in sextains, i.e. iambic pentametre quatrain followed by a couplet and Shakespeare shows himself to be a master of this form. Many such poems were being written at this time and Shakespeare had models enough to guide him. Though it was a new field for him, he takes up the form of "erotic epyllion" and shows himself to be a master at it. He is as much at home in drama as in the form of a lyrical and sensuous love-story in a complex stanza-pattern.

The Rape of Lucrece

This was published in the year following that of his first narrative poem, *Venus and Adonis*. This, too, like the former, is based on classical myths, and, like the former, was dedicated to the Earl of Southampton. The stanza-form is more complex than that used in the former. It is in rhyme royal, a stanza of seven iambic pentametre lines in an intricate rhyme-scheme. The figure of Tarquin is presented with great psychological insight so that he becomes a tragic character. This complexity raises the poem far above the level of a merely well-written and entertaining story. The poet's own personality shines through the classical panoply.

The Sonnets

The love-sonnet sequence was one of the most popular poetic forms of the time and Shakespeare uses the prevailing fashion to write one of his most intensely emotional works. It is a sequence of a hundred and fifty-four sonnets. The entire sequence is dedicated to "the onlie begetter" Mr. W.H. who is not named more specifically. The majority of the sonnets are addressed to him and the rest to an equally mysterious Dark Lady. Many were the sequences produced at that time, but none of them can approach Shakespeare's in intensity of emotion or in the beauty of expression.

Titus Andronicus

This is a revenge tragedy in the Senecan tradition which was popularised by Kyd. It is a typical blood-and-thunder tragedy supplying exactly what the audience wanted, but too crude for modern tastes. Kyd's *The Spanish Tragedy* guided Shakespeare as far as the technique and the theme of revenge are concerned, but it is clear that our poet is not influenced by Kyd's bombastic rhetoric. In fact he parodies a famous passage in Kyd's play, beginning "O eyes no eyes but fountains full of tears". The play was immensely popular at the time. The atrocities in the story have been made tolerable by being placed in ancient Rome.

Richard II

Topical relevance is a limiting factor in any work and Shakespeare's works are universal rather than topical. Yet the theme of this play was such that in the Elizabethan times it had topical relevance. Queen Elizabeth, seeing it, had angrily exclaimed: "I am Richard II, know ye that?... This tragedy is played forty times in open streets and houses". The king had divine rights, and his deposition was a highly sensitive issue. When the play was staged, all the scenes dealing with the deposition of King Richard II had to be omitted. It is thought that the play is a study in weakness of character in the person of the hero, Richard II.

A Midsummer Night's Dream

This charming comedy has been hailed as his best early comedy. It is a fantasy in which fairies take active part in the action and influence human beings. It has been claimed for Shakespeare that it was he who, in this play, created the new genre of fairy-tale comedy and he will use it again in his last play *The Tempest*. The art of characterisation is a special feature of this play, for three levels of characters have been presented in it: the fairies, the two pairs of romantic aristocratic lovers, and the robust earthy villagers. Bottom the weaver, of this last group, is the strongest portrayal and has passed into immortality.

Love's Labour's Lost

This play is notable for its dialogue of sparkling wit. He uses a host of courtly characters in it, all talking in highly polished language. Humbler characters are also present. A short passage of this play has become specially well-known. The merriest and wittiest of the lords, Lord Berowne, decides to give up ornate and witty diction ("taffeta phrases, silken terms precise") and adopt a simpler mode of speaking ("russet yeas and honest kersey noes."). Lord Berowne is supposed to be a slightly autobiographical character. The theme of love and marriage is treated here with great gusto and good-humour, the poet poking fun at the lords.

King John

This play contains a curious paradox in it. It is an entirely historical play, yet it has topical relevance as well. In this play, religion is an important issue, exactly as it was in those days. King John, just like Queen Elizabeth, carried on a lifelong struggle with the Pope. The focus of interest, however, is not religion, though it is an important issue. The play, therefore, cannot be called a religious play. It is, on the other hand, a historical play and essentially patriotic. The relationship with foreign powers is the central theme of the play, and this was one of the living issues of his own times as well.

The Merchant of Venice

This is the first of the group of the four romantic comedies, also known as the golden or the happy comedies. The merchant after whom the play is named is Antonio, yet he cannot be called the hero. The position of the most important character is taken by Shylock—a character who is a class by himself. The heroine Portia is one of the most important female characters of our poet. The Elizabethan stage-convention of disguise is used most effectively in the play, for all the three female characters in it adopt disguises. His poetic style has come to a high standard of excellence in it.

Henry IV, Parts 1 and 2

These two plays can be said to have taken the history play to a high peak of excellence not reached since then. Sir John Falstaff has become the very epitome of a comic character. Even Shakespeare's own later creation Sir Toby of *Twelfth Night* pales by comparison. The play, though the comic scenes steal the limelight, is about the serious issues of the duties of and the responsibilities of kings. The second part of the play emphasizes the theme. This is seen the best in the rejection-scene in which King Henry V rejects Falstaff. As Prince Hal, he had been a carefree young man, but when he becomes the king, he will have to bid farewell to his former life. So, Falstaff is rejected in one of the most moving scenes.

The Merry Wives of Windsor

Falstaff had so captivated Queen Elizabeth that she specially ordered a play on "the fat knight in love." Thus, this play came to be written. This play begins at the point where *Henry IV*, Pt. 2 ends. It is a boisterous farce, the only such play Shakespeare had written. It is a simple, laughter-provoking play, not a humorous satire. This is a feature to be noted because one of the characters in it, Corporal Nym, is supposed to be a parody of a humour character. By this time, Ben Jonson had started to write his highly successful humour comedies and Nym is such a character.

King Henry V

Just as the three parts of *Henry VI*, together with *Richard III*, make up a tetralogy, so do *Richard III*, the two *Henry IV* parts and this play. *King Henry V* presents Shakespeare's concept of the ideal king. The two dominant themes of the play are those of patriotism and the duties of kingship. The famous battle of Agincourt is presented in an entirely impartial manner—with its heroism and nobility as well as its cruelty and bloodshed. The young king is presented as the ideal leader of men in the field of battle, but later when the battle comes to an end he is the ideal king who knows how to temper justice with mercy.

Much Ado About Nothing

This play is a romantic comedy and belongs to the group of the golden or the happy comedies: Like all of them, this play also revolves around the central theme of love. This theme is presented in many different ways in this play. The Hero-Claudio plot gives physical love based on appearances, the Benedick-Beatrice plot presents the rejection of married love. The theme of love versus friendship is also presented as in *The Two Gentlemen of Verona*. Shakespeare's expertise in the management of plot is also evident, for there is a clear-cut main plot and another subsidiary plot. This clarity of outline is absent in *The Merchant of Venice*.

Julius Caesar

This is a Roman tragedy. The play is a purely political one and takes up the theme of the conflict between tyranny and liberty. The story is taken from Lord North's translation of Plutarch's *Lives*. It was highly successful on the stage. The Forum Scene with Mark Antony's famous speech is one of the highlights of the play. Shakespeare makes use of the supernatural element in the form of Julius Caesar's ghost. This is so important an element that scholars and critics have opined that Caesar's ghost casts a shadow over the entire play as the Ghost in *Hamlet* does.

As You Like It

This is avowedly the best of the golden comedies. More than half of the play is located in the pastoral environment of the forest of Arden and this has led to its being labelled as a pastoral comedy. Love, the central theme as in all romantic comedies, is presented in four different ways through four pairs of lovers. There are royal and courtly characters as well as humble shepherds. At the end of the play all are neatly paired off, with four marriages in the play. Rosalind is one of the most charming heroines and her use of a male disguise produces some effective examples of dramatic irony.

Twelfth Night

In this, the last of the golden comedies, the main theme is love and two different aspects of it have been dealt with. A later and paler counterpart of Falstaff is present in the person of Sir Toby. It also contains one of the most famous clowns of Shakespeare in the character of Feste. Shakespeare rarely used humour characters in his plays, but this play contains one such—Malvolio the melancholy Puritan. The heroine Viola, like the heroines of the three other golden comedies, adopts a male disguise and retains it for longer than any other heroine. The play takes up the theme of mistaken identities which was one of the first themes used by Shakespeare, in *The Comedy of Errors*. He has taken the story from many different sources.

Hamlet

This is the last of his plays written in the Elizabethan period. It is also the first of the group of the four great tragedies and ushers in a period of dark mood in Shakespeare's artistic career. It is basically a revenge tragedy, but the character of Hamlet has gained so much importance that this feature has receded into the background. Nothing can prove the supremacy of Shakespeare more than the manner in which he has taken up the crude melodramatic form of the blood-and-thunder revenge tragedy and lifted it up to the heights of deep psychological complexity. It contains all the elements of a revenge tragedy, but soars up high beyond the limitations of one.

Troilus and Cressida

In this play, Shakespeare goes far back in time and space for inspiration—to the world of Greek myths. This is the first of the problem comedies. These plays like the tragedies, deal with the problem of evil, but do not end tragically. The entire atmosphere is a dark and gloomy one and the plays are thus also known as the dark comedies. This play is thought to be Shakespeare's nearest approach to satire. There is a famous speech in the play, known as the degree speech, delivered by Ulysses who is a character known for his wisdom. It is thought that his speeches echo the thoughts of the dramatist himself.

All's Well that Ends Well

This play, like *Troilus and Cressida*, belongs to the group of problem comedies, but it is not so satirical as the former. The main plot, concerning Bertram and Helena, expounds the theme of the conflict between virtue and nobility. Apart from these, there are many other sub-themes, like the hollowness of romantic love. Deception and mistaken identity are used as a basis for marriage. Rejection of devoted love is also one of the themes, for Bertram's rejection forces Helena to deceive him. The change in Shakespeare's attitude to life is seen most clearly in the figure of the satirical portrait of the braggart soldier, Parolles, who is totally different from the lovable Falstaff.

Measure for Measure

The third of the problem comedies, it is a very bitter play. The paradox is that this extremely gloomy comedy resembles *As You Like It,* the happiest of the happy comedies, in one respect—both end with no less than four marriages. Here also, as in *All's Well That Ends Well*, there is the theme of rejection of love. In addition there is the serious issue of justice and its administration, which is one of the important themes in his later plays. This also involves the social issues of morality and the law, and the religious issues of sin and grace. The seriousness of the poet's attitude is always in evidence.

Othello

This is the first of the tragedies performed in Jacobean times and is often called "the *Romeo and Juliet* of the later Shakespeare". It is also juxtaposed with the later Romance *The Winter's Tale*, as both the plays give us studies in jealousy. Othello, the hero presents the destructive effects of jealousy. There is also the figure of Iago which has puzzled the Shakespearean scholars because he brings about the tragic end by sowing the seeds of jealousy in Othello's mind for no discernible reason. Coleridge's famous phrase "motiveless malignity" describes Iago most aptly.

King Lear

This is his next work and is acknowledged to be the greatest of his tragedies. It has been called a "cosmic drama".

Macbeth

This is taken to be Shakespeare's gloomiest play and is the fourth of the great tragedies. He has portrayed a Scottish hero as a compliment to King James. This can be classed as a Conqueror tragedy. This tragedy gives us the unique figure of Lady Macbeth, which is all the more remarkable as tragedies are hero-centred plays. She overshadows all but Macbeth. This play is also remarkable in that it makes use of the Three Witches whose prophecies are instrumental in bringing about the tragic end.

Antony and Cleopatra

This is classed as a Roman tragedy and depicts the events following *Julius Caesar*. As such it can be regarded as a sequel to it. It shows Mark Antony's life after the battle at Philippi. Caesar's empire was divided into three parts among the three members of the Triumvirate and Egypt had fallen to Mark Antony's share. He then goes to Egypt and meets Cleopatra. Thus the theme of love as an all-consuming and all-compensating factor is introduced. It is a historical tragedy on the theme of love and had inspired Dryden's *All for Love*.

Coriolanus

This too is classed, with *Julius Caesar* and *Antony and Cleopatra*, as a Roman tragedy. The theme of honour versus popularity is taken up here. The hero is a man of such nobility that he cannot stoop to make himself cheap in order to win popularity. This obstinacy brings about his tragic doom.

Timon of Athens

Classed among the problem comedies, this play had never been staged. It is now accepted by many scholars as an unfinished play, though at a superficial reading it seems to be a complete one. The last part of the play shows the misanthropic hero's withdrawal from society, and this gives the play some completeness.

Pericles

This is the first play of the last phase. He takes up the theme of sin and repentance which leads to forgiveness and to regeneration. This is the theme of all the last romances. It will recur, with variations, in all the last plays. All these plays have a rather unrealistic fairy-tale atmosphere which has led to their being grouped together as romances.

Cymbeline

This is the second play of the last group, treating the same theme as *Pericles*. Imogen, the heroine, dons a male disguise as the heroines of his earlier plays do. King Cymbeline, like Pericles, loses his children, but gets them back after long years of separation and repentance, as is the case with all the last romances.

The Winter's Tale

This play is often coupled with *Othello* as being a study in jealousy. In addition, it has all the other features of the last Romances. This play is well-known as being the most notorious violation of the classical rules of the Unities, particularly that of time, for it covers more than sixteen years. It contains some of the most charming pastoral scenes in Shakespeare. The theme of sin and repentance and forgiveness is to be found here as in all the last Romances. Leontes is one of his important male figures.

The Tempest

This is the last of the Romances and our poet's last play as well. It is thought that the figure of the wise Prospero is faintly autobiographical. The play was staged to celebrate a royal betrothal and it is thought that the poet himself acted in the role of Prospero. The same theme is taken up as in all the last romances and Miranda is a symbol of purity, innocence and virtue, more so than any other heroine.

Henry VIII

This play belongs to the cycle of chronicle plays, but it is different from them in that it discusses an important theme—patience in adversity. Not only the King but the other characters also have to learn this. The authorship of this play has for long been in doubt.

The Two Noble Kinsmen

This is a dramatisation of *The Knight's Tale* as told by Chaucer and was written in collaboration with Fletcher. The major parts of Act I, III and V were by Shakespeare. Then Fletcher introduced a vulgar sub-plot which was out of tune with the solemnity of the main plot concerning Palamon and Arcite. This displeased Shakespeare and he refused to collaborate any further with Fletcher.

NOTES

1. Irving Ribner, *William Shakespeare: Life, Times and Theatre*. London: John Wiley & Sons Inc., 1969, p. 31.
2. Cited in F.E. Halliday, *The Life of Shakespeare*. London: Gerald Duckworth & Co. Ltd., 1961, p. 20.
3. I. Ribner, *op. cit.*, p. 38.
4. F.E. Halliday, *op. cit.*, p. 59.
5. Quoted in Ribner, *op. cit.*, p. 45.
6. A.L. Rowse, *William Shakespeare: A Biography*. London: Macmillan & Co. Ltd., 1963, p. 201.
7. Halliday, *op. cit.*, p. 118.
8. *Ibid.*, p. 138.
9. *Ibid.*, p. 183.
10. Quoted in I. Ribner, *op. cit.*, p. 64.

3

The Story and the Genre

(a) The Story in Brief

Julius Caesar recounts the events surrounding the assassination of Julius Caesar. As he is a historical person, Shakespeare had to follow the actual history quite closely. How much he deviated from historical truth handed down to posterity (if and when he deviated at all) and what interpretation he put upon them will be discussed in the relevant chapter. Here the story as given in the play is being recounted.

The play opens on the day of the feast of Lupercalia, an ancient Roman religious festival. Caesar has come back triumphant after his battle in Spain with the sons of Pompey and wants to make the festival an occasion for celebrating his own triumph. This is resented intensely by many of the aristocratic and influential men of Rome, who think that Caesar is getting rather too ambitious. They fear that he may go in for absolute monarchy.

This apprehension is partially borne out at what happens during the feast. Mark Antony offers Caesar the crown in front of a big crowd and Caesar refuses it. This happens, not once, but three times. Every time the crowd cheers and Brutus and Cassius think that this is only the beginning, that Caesar will seize power sooner or later. Cassius belongs to a group of conspirators who want to overthrow Caesar and they want to have Brutus in their group. Brutus is Caesar's friend, and anyway he does not want to join the conspirators in the beginning, but Caesar's own attitude gradually changes his mind. Directly after refusing the crown Caesar enters the stage and his words indicate that he regards himself as superior to everyone. All this makes Brutus, after much searching of heart, join the conspiracy.

This happens on the day before the ides of March (i.e. the fifteenth). This is extremely significant because, on the day of the feast a soothsayer had warned Caesar that the ides of March would be dangerous for him and that he should be especially careful on that day. On the eve of the ides, Brutus joins the conspirators and then and there they decide to kill Caesar. The other conspirators, especially Cassius want that Antony should also be killed, but Brutus thinks it will be needless bloodshed to do so. Brutus is a man of unimpeachable integrity and great nobility, so he does not want to kill anyone whose death is not absolutely necessary for the future of Rome:

> Our course will seem too bloody, Caius Cassius,
> To cut the head off and then hack the limbs,
> Like wrath in death and envy afterwards;
> For Antony is but a limb of Caesar.[1]

The sentiments are noble ones and just the right kind of sentiments for a man like Brutus. All the same, this was a serious mistake, because Mark Antony is extremely loyal to Caesar and he will bring about civil war in the country. For the present, however, the conspirators agree with Brutus. After they go away Portia, Brutus's wife, comes and pleads with him to confide in her for he has been behaving rather oddly and she has suspicions that something has disturbed him. Before Brutus can confide in her, there is an interruption and he goes away to meet Caesar.

The day that has now dawned after the night of conspiracy, is the fateful ides of March and though the priests as well as Calpurnia tell him not to go out to speak to the Senate, Caesar decides he will go to the Capitol. The priests have made a sacrifice and send him the message that the omens are bad. Calpurnia also had had an ominous dream and pleads with him not to go out. At first Caesar decides that he will not go, but allows himself to be persuaded by Decius to go out.

Decius belongs to the group of conspirators and advises him in their interest. He holds out the bait that the Senate has decided to confer the crown upon him and this Caesar cannot resist.

In front of the Capitol as well as within the Senate several persons bring their suits and Caesar behaves as if he were already the king. This does but serve to confirm the resolution of the conspirators and they stab him to death. Brutus had been in front of him and when he stabs Caesar, Caesar can hardly believe it:

> Et tu, Brute—Then fall Caesar.[2]

These are the last words of Caesar and he dies immediately after. The assassination occurs in the middle of the play:

> At the play's formal and thematic heart is corpse—the dead Caesar—on stage for some 200 lines in the middle of the play and remains in the minds of the characters throughout.[3]

Brutus then pacifies and reassures the apprehensive senators and then occurs the blood-bath scene. Brutus makes everyone dip his hands in Caesar's blood:

> Stoop, Romans, stoop,
> And let us bathe our hands in Caesar's blood
> Up to the elbows, and besmear our swords:
> Then walk we forth, even to the market place,
> And waving our red weapons o'er our heads,
> Let's all cry, "Peace, freedom, and liberty"![4]

They thus wash their hands in Caesar's blood and then Antony sends a message wanting to meet them and promise allegiance. When he comes, he pretends to be on their side and extracts a promise from Brutus that he will be allowed to deliver a funeral oration on Caesar. This is another grave mistake on Brutus's part, for as soon as Antony is left alone with the dead body of Caesar he makes his allegiance clear and vows revenge.

In the famous Forum speech, Antony acts as a mere rabble-rouser. War has to be declared. Brutus with the conspirators and Antony with the support of Octavius and Lepidus muster their armies.

Unfortunately, for the Republicans, Cassius and Brutus have a serious quarrel before the battle. They accuse each other and a compromise is reached only after they realize that they cannot afford to go against each other at this juncture. Brutus also tells Cassius of Portia's death and this softens Cassius's heart.

It is decided that the battle will take place at Philippi and after this decision, the others go away, leaving Brutus alone. He is very tired and wants to sleep, but it is now that the Ghost of Caesar comes. He is there for a very short time and tells Brutus that he is Brutus's evil spirit. After declaring twice that he shall meet Brutus at Philippi he vanishes. Brutus is extremely perturbed, especially when he realizes that he is the only one who has seen the Ghost.

The outcome of the battle is disastrous for the Republicans. Antony's army is victorious. Almost everyone dies. Those who do not die fighting, like Cassius, Titinius and Brutus, commit suicide. Taking one's own life is an unforgiveable sin according to the Christian doctrine, but not according to the ancient Roman religion. It is an act of honour. Antony pays homage to Brutus and the play ends.

(b) The Genre of the Play

There have been many debates and differences of opinion over each aspect of Shakespeare's plays. This one is a quite straightforward play, dealing with historical figures and historical incidents, yet there has been difference of opinion over its genre. It has been called a Roman tragedy, a historical tragedy, a tragedy of revenge, a political tragedy, etc. A few of these views will be discussed now.

(i) Tragical History or Historical Tragedy

A.C. Bradley differentiates the play from "pure tragedy" and calls it "tragical history or historical tragedy". He puts within this group not only the Roman plays but two English chronicle plays also:

> *Richard III* and *Richard II*, *Julius Caesar, Antony and Cleopatra* and *Coriolanus* are tragical histories or historical tragedies, in which Shakespeare acknowledges

in practice a certain obligation to follow his authorities, even when that authority offers him an undramatic material.[5]

It is a fact that Shakespeare had to follow, more or less faithfully, historical facts handed down to posterity by renowned historians that differentiates this play from the other tragedies, like *Hamlet*, *Othello*, *Lear or Macbeth*. In these and other tragedies Shakespeare followed many sources like old plays, narrative poems, romances, etc. and modified his materials according to his dramatic needs. They also follow the accepted pattern of tragedies and the classical rules can be applied to them though Shakespeare did not follow the rules at all strictly. With the plays designated by Bradley as historical tragedy, however, this is not the case. Here there are well-known historical facts and the dramatist has to follow them. The characters also are well-known historical figures and he has, more or less, to portray them as such. So these plays are different from "pure" tragedies and the usual classical rules applicable to tragedies should not be applied to them. Bradley thinks that Shakespeare himself must have thought along these lines:

> Probably he himself would have met some critic to whom these plays are open by appealing to their historical character and by denying that such works are to be judged by the standard of pure tragedies.[6]

As the standards of pure tragedy should not be applied to such plays, Bradley has not written at length about *Julius Caesar*. He, however, concedes that these tragedies often show deviations from those standards and therefore the rules applied to pure tragedies can be applied with modifications to these historical tragedies also. Though he has not devoted individual chapters on this play he refers to it no less than nineteen times while discussing the other plays and particularly the general principles of tragedy. A few of his valuable opinions will now be mentioned, though not discussed in detail.

The very first point he takes up about tragedy is that of the hero. He points out that the play is centred around one or sometimes two characters:

> ...it is pre-eminently the story of one person, the "hero", or at most of two, the "hero" and the "heroine".[7]

Though here he is talking about the principles of pure tragedy, he does not forget a work like *Julius Caesar* and in an extremely pithy sentence points out many features of this play:

> *Julius Caesar* is not an exception to this rule. Caesar, whose murder comes in the Third Act, is in a sense the dominant figure in the story, but Brutus is the "hero".[8]

In other words, this play is like the other tragedies in this respect and therefore, can validly claim the status of a tragedy, and not be regarded as just a historical play. Then he implies that since the play is named after Caesar, he should rightly be regarded as the hero, and points out that his murder comes in the middle of the play, which should not happen in a proper tragedy since one of the classical requirements is that the hero should be present in the play throughout. Who, then, should be named the hero? Bradley gives this status to Brutus, but at the same time declares that Caesars's is the dominant figure in the play.

Since both Caesar and Brutus are historical figures and both die, we can say that the designation "historical tragedy" fits *Julius Caesar*.

Another extremely important element of tragedy is conflict. This can occur at many levels. There can be conflicts between countries or within them. Bradley mentions this factor of "outward conflict", but does not comment upon its presence in this play. He is more interested in inner conflict:

> There is an outward conflict of persons and groups, there is also a conflict of forces in the hero's soul; and even in *Julius Caesar* and *Macbeth* the intensity of the former can hardly be said to exceed that of the latter.[9]

From this point of view, Brutus can truly be called the hero of the play. Caesar is full of arrogant self-confidence. There is a little amount of conflict of a very superficial kind in him when he debates whether to go out on the ides of March or not. This conflict is there for a very short time. At first he is determined to go! "Caesar shall go forth", then, as he is superstitious, the priests' omens and Calpurnia's dreams together with the soothsayer's warning, makes him hesitate:

> Mark Antony shall say I am not well
> And for thy humour I will stay at home
> … … …
> I will not come today. Tell them so, Decius.[10]

Then when Decius persuades him to the contrary, he changes his mind again. So the conflict is short-lived.

The conflict in Brutus's mind is of a far more serious kind. He is torn by conflict from the very beginning till the end (*vide* chap. 7 *infra* for more details). Thus again, from the point of view of conflict, both outer and inner ones, *Julius Caesar* can be called a tragedy, and since these conflicts are historically true, it is a historical tragedy.

These are but two of the basic rules of tragedy which can be applied to this play. Bradley gives several other examples throughout his work to justify the label he has chosen for this play.

(ii) Political Melodrama

This is the opinion of Shaw. He takes Shakespeare seriously as a dramatist but refuses to take *Julius Caesar* seriously. In fact he denigrates the characters and the plot and makes it clear that both are all right for a melodrama but cannot be considered to have the high seriousness of tragedy:

> *Julius Caesar*, the most splendidly written political melodrama we possess….
>
> Regarded as a crafty stage job, the play is a triumph: rhetoric, claptrap, effective gushes of emotion, all the devices of the popular playwright, are employed with a profusion of power that almost breaks their backs.[11]

Shaw, in other words, makes Shakespeare out to be writing a play in the Scribean manner as he himself did. What he says may be partially true, but it does not account for the undoubted feeling of tragic dignity and tragic equilibrium that the play produces. Shaw himself was not able to write a tragedy and cannot appreciate the effect produced by the play.

(iii) Revenge Tragedy

This is a far more justifiable label than that given by Shaw and can be said to be partially applicable to the play as the motif of revenge is introduced in the middle of the play. Antony, when left alone with the dead body of Caesar, is motivated by the desire for revenge:

> Woe to the hand that shed this costly blood!
> Over thy wounds now do I prophesy
> ... ...
> A curse shall light upon the limbs of men
> Domestic fury and fierce civil strife
> Shall cumber all the parts of Italy;
> ... ... And Caesar's spirit, ranging for revenge,
> And Ate by his side come hot from hell.[12]

This, as Norman Rabkin points out, refers specifically to the tradition of revenge tragedy:

> No member of an audience—remembering the *Ur Hamlet* and *Titus Andronicus*, still in love with *The Spanish Tragedy* and within a year of seeing the first performance of *Hamlet*, could have missed Shakespeare's points.[13]

This critic is of the opinion that the play takes the course of a revenge tragedy when Brutus makes the conspirators bathe their hands in Caesar's blood. Indeed, from Antony's speech onwards, the play contains all the ingredients of a revenge tragedy. Antony is the revenger, eager to avenge the murder of Caesar. As in Kyd's *The Spanish Tragedy* and in Webster's *The Duchess of Malfi* the innocent victim is killed in the middle of the play. It is true that Caesar is ambitious and not quite as innocent as Horatio in the former play and the Duchess in the latter, but it cannot be denied that he had not harmed anyone. As is the requirement of a revenge play, the Ghost of Caesar appears in this play also. It is not necessary that the Ghost of the victim should incite the revenger as the elder Hamlet's Ghost does. He can be just a passive onlooker as the Ghost of Andrea is in Kyd's play. Here however, the Ghost comes midway between Kyd's and Hamlet's, for he is not as passive as the former though not as active as the latter. He comes to warn Brutus and make him and the audience aware of the wrong that has been done to him.

Another feature of revenge tragedies as pointed out by Helen Gardner is that, often enough, the wrongdoer (who is to be revenged upon) furnishes the revenger with the means for revenge:

> The revenger takes an opportunity unconsciously provided for him by the villain. Given this opportunity... he forms his schemes on the spur of the moment.[14]

In Kyd's play, the opportunity to enact a play is given to Hicronymo by Lorenzo and in *Hamlet* the opportunity for the fatal duel is given to Hamlet by Claudius. Here the same thing happens in that Antony is given the opportunity to deliver a funeral oration by Brutus himself and takes full advantage of the chance thus given to him. Again, one of the requirements of a revenge tragedy is that the motivation for revenge has to be strong enough to justify the revenger and gain him the sympathy of the reader or the audience:

> The revenger of the drama started with the sympathy of the audience if his cause were good and if he acted according to the typical English notion of straightforward fair play.[15]

Here, more than half the battle is won because the characters are not Christians. It is in the Christian religion that revenge has been forbidden, but this play takes place in pagan times when Christian ethics did not apply. Besides, the manner of killing Caesar and especially the blood-bath would make the reader sympathetic towards Antony.

Taking all these factors into account, the play can be designated as a revenge tragedy, though the term can be only partially applied to it. It is the second half of the play that can be designated as such. Rabkin, though it is he who has expounded the idea, also recognizes this fact:

> The action of the play makes clear sense in terms of revenge tragedy. From the moment of the murder Brutus

> is marked out as victim, and historical process will operate on the principle that blood will have blood.[16]

The relevance of this remark becomes even more clear when another of the notable features of the revenge tragedy is considered. A significant fact about them is that the revenger himself does not create the circumstances that call for revenge—the situation is thrust upon him:

> The essence of any tragedy of revenge is that its hero has not created the situation in which he finds himself and out of which the tragedy arises.[17]

This is exactly what happens in our play. After the assassination, Antony is confronted with the fact. He had nothing to do with it—the situation has been thrust upon him. He very clearly and cleverly conceals his true allegiance and expresses it only in his soliloquy, but the fact remains that this could not have happened till the murder had been accomplished and therefore it is from then onwards that the action veers towards that of a revenge play.

It is largely because of this that the question of morality has become so important in *Julius Caesar*. The revenger, in searching out the swiftest and the most effective way of having his revenge, disregards morality. As Rabkin points out:

> Morality is irrelevant: the efficient revenger must dissemble, disclaiming the very rhetoric he employs, urging indiscriminate mischief to take what course it will.[18]

Thus, for Antony, the question of morality is quite irrelevant. It is also not an effective question for, as has been pointed out, Christian ethics does not apply here. In this play the question of morality centres around Brutus, on whom the play depends.

It should be noted that Bullough does not agree with the view that the play is a revenge play. He very pertinently points out that whereas in such a play the wrongdoer should not have any claims on the reader's sympathy, that does not happen in this. Our sympathy is not alienated from Brutus and Cassius. Shakespeare has, indeed, portrayed all characters in such a manner that we respect all of them. The conduct of the victorious leaders, Antony and Cassius, commands our admiration:

> That Shakespeare wished to avoid writing just another tragedy of revenge...is made clear, for sympathy with Brutus and Cassius, if shaken, is not lost.[19]

(iv) Tragedy of Moral Choice

Virgil K. Whitaker thinks that in *Julius Caesar* Shakespeare is dramatising a moral choice. In this he has followed the tradition of the native English morality plays:

> There is a similar progress in dramatic technique from the moralities through *Faust* to *Julius Caesar*.[20]

This critic thus takes a very serious view of the play, regarding it as, if not a morality play, definitely a play in that tradition. He regards Marlowe as presenting the spiritual biography of a scholar driven by the sin of despair to ultimate damnation and conjectures that Shakespeare developed his technique from the first soliloquy of Dr. Faustus:

> Since Shakespeare probably borrowed his technique in *Julius Caesar* from this soliloquy, it is worth examining.[21]

Whitaker then focuses on Brutus's famous soliloquy in Act II, sc. i and presents the dilemma that Brutus faces in it. He calls Brutus's character a noble one, but the choice he made is a "false choice" because it ultimately leads to civil war. Tracing the history of a choice of moral issues, he goes back to Greek tragedy, mentioning Antigone's defiance of Creon. Thus the matter of moral choice is not at all new, whether in classical drama or English. The novelty of Shakespeare's attitude lay in another direction:

> What is new is the attempt to make the act of choice an important part of the play and to work it out in detail according to accepted psychological theory.[22]

According to him, Shakespeare, through *Julius Caesar*, worked out a certain formula for a tragedy of moral choice. The expository part of the play serves: (a) the dilemma which the hero faces is explained. In *Julius Caesar* it is Cassius who presents the choice to Brutus, (b) the actual choice is made in Brutus's soliloquy, (c) a decisive step is taken, that is, Caesar's assassination. This formula applies not only to *Julius Caesar* but to other plays like *Othello, King Lear, Antony and Cleopatra*, etc. but Shakespeare used it for the first time in this one.

Taking a less technical and more generalized view of the moral choice theme, H.S. Wilson thinks in this play, political tragedy and moral tragedy go hand in hand. Moreover, Whitaker focuses on Brutus in considering the play as a moral play, but Wilson extends the problem of morality to Caesar as well:

> This political tragedy involves as a consequence the moral tragedy of Brutus; and Brutus's moral tragedy, in turn, is mirrored in Caesar's, for Brutus's act is no better justified in its outcome than Caesar's aims, perhaps less justified.[23]

(v) Problem Play

This view of the play is very different from that of Shakespeare's own Problem Comedies or Shaw's Problem plays. Ernest Schanzer classes it, along with plays like *Measure for Measure* and *Troilus and Cressida* as a Problem play and means by that term that Shakespeare explained certain problems in it. He highlights the character of Brutus and the role he plays. Brutus is a man torn by conflicts, who makes a disastrous choice that brings ruin and destruction. The problem Shakespeare deals with and embodies in the person of Brutus is:

> How far may the politician or citizen alike go when called upon to act when things are desperately on the slide?[24]

Schanzer analyses the character of Brutus and shows that he is a self-deceived man and acts through the best of motives in a totally wrong manner:

> Instead of benefiting his country, Brutus has, from the best of motives and the highest principles, plunged it into ruin.[25]

The problem that such a man and his action raises, the problem of carrying out one's responsibilities for the sake of saving or improving the state of one's country, is raised, but not solved. This critic implies that it is this lack of a fitting solution of the problem raised is deliberate on Shakespeare's part and it is this that makes it a problem play.

Not many critics would agree with this view of the play and of the view that Schanzer takes of Shakespeare's presentation of the two chief characters. He argues that both Caesar and Brutus are presented as rather ambivalent characters and that is the main source of the problem of the justifiability of the murder of one by the other. Bullough, for one, refuses to regard the play as a problem play:

> The play is not a "problem play" in the sense that we are left undecided how to regard the characters. The ambivalence of presentation is not intended to confuse or offer alternative interpretation.[26]

Julius Caesar is one of the most straightforward plays of Shakespeare. Yet Shakespeare's plays are so complex that a great variety of interpretations is available on every aspect of his plays. Only a few of such interpretation on the aspect of the genre of the play have been given here. In addition to these it has also been called a Political Tragedy, a Roman Play, the Tragedy of Brutus, etc. This great variety of opinions on the comparatively simple aspect of its genre will serve to make the complexity of the play clear to everyone. The diligent student should not allow them to bewilder him. As we delve deeper into the play, different aspects of it will come to the fore and the complexity of the play will become more and more clear. Every age has added its own quota to the opinions of the critics and the twentieth century, with its great wealth of serious critical study, has given, so far, the most varied opinions.

NOTES

1. T.S. Dorsch, ed., *Julius Caesar*, the Arden Shakespeare series, New Delhi, B.I. Pubs, 1981. Act II, sc.ii, lines 162-65, p. 42. All future citations from the text of *JC* will be from this edn.
2. Act III, sc. i, line 77, p. 67.

3. Emma Smith, Introduction *JC*, Ware, Worsworth Classics, 1992, p. 6.
4. Act III, sc. i, lines 105-10, p. 69.
5. A.C. Bradley, *Shakespearean Tragedy*, London, Macmillan and Co. Ltd., 1960, p. xv.
6. *Ibid.*
7. *Ibid.*, p. 2.
8. *Ibid.*
9. *Ibid.*, pp. 11-12.
10. Act II, sc. ii, ll. 55-56, p. 64.
11. Peter Ure, *Shakespeare: Julius Caesar*. The Casebook series, Bristol, Macmillan, 1969, p. 40.
12. Act III, sc. i, ll 258-71, p. 76.
13. Ure, *op. cit.*, p. 104.
14. Helen Gardner, *The Historical Approach to Hamlet*, in John Jump, ed., *Hamlet: A Casebook*, Houndmills, Palgraccue, 1968, p. 142.
15. F.T. Bowers, *Elizabethan Revenge Tragedy*, Princeton, Princeton Univ. Pr., 1940, p. 40.
16. Ure, *op. cit.*, p. 105.
17. Gardner, *op. cit.*, p. 141.
18. Rabkin, *op. cit.*, p. 105.
19. Geoffrey Bullough, Narrative and Dramatic Sources of Shakespeare, Vol. V, London, Routledge and Kegan Paul, 1966, p. 56.
20. Virgil K. Whitaker, *Brutus and the Tragedy of Moral Choice*, in Ure, *op. cit.*, p. 172.
21. *Ibid.*, p. 173.
22. *Ibid.*, p. 178.
23. H.S. Wilson, *On the Design of Shakespeare's Tragedy*, Univ. of Toronto Pr., 1968, p. 89.
24. Ure, *op.cit.*, p. 24.
25. E. Schanzer, *The Tragedy of Brutus*, Ure, *op. cit.*, p. 193.
26. Bullough, *op. cit.*, p. 57.

4

A Scene-wise Analysis

Act I, sc. i

The opening scene of the play is a dynamic street scene. There are two tribunes talking to some artisans. They are in a holiday mood and are not working. Nor are they wearing the kind of clothes that would identify their trades; instead, they have their holiday dresses on. Flavius and Marullus, after rebuking a carpenter and cobbler for not working, ask them what kind of holiday is it that they are enjoying. The cobbler answers that they are going to celebrate Caesar's triumph.

Caesar has recently defeated Gnaeus and Sextus, sons of Pompey, in Spain, and come back to Rome. It is this victory that is going to be celebrated but the two tribunes resent the fact. They admired Pompey and see no cause to celebrate Caesar's victory. This fact is given in Shakespeare's source, Lord North's translation of Plutarch's *Lives*:

> But the triumph he made into Rome for the same did as much offend the Romans, and more, than anything he had ever done before: because he had not overcome captains that were strangers, nor barbarous kings, but had destroyed the sons of the noblest man of Rome.[1]

Marullus makes his attitude clear in a speech and tells the plebeians to go home. The two tribunes then proceed to remove all trophies and ornaments from the statues of Caesar standing in the city.

Here, we come to know that it is the day of the religious festival of Lupercalia and Marullus has misgivings about disrobing the images on such a day. Flavius however persuades him to do so. They decide that they will clear the streets of people and also disrobe Caesar's statue. In other words they are determined to make the celebrations fail, for they think that celebrating Caesar's triumph will give him undue importance:

> These glowing feathers pluck'd from Caesar's wings
> Will make him fly an ordinary pitch,
> Who else would soar above the view of men
> And keep us all in servile fearfulness.[2]

As there is no separate prologue to the play, this scene has to be treated as a prologue. Usually in classical plays the prologue tells the part of the story that has taken place before the play begins, and also part of the story that is going to be presented, but the Elizabethans put it to other uses also. Here in this scene Shakespeare gives the background of the play and also a clear indication of Caesar's unpopularity with the aristocracy of Rome. In addition Shakespeare also makes us realize the fickleness of the populace of Rome. They are in a cheerful holiday mood, but the minute two noblemen tell them to go home they do so at once, without voicing any objections. As a substitude for a Prologue, thus, the scene is a successful one:

> The opening scene of a Shakespearean play has always a peculiar significance....not merely in virtue of its providing a convenient and effective starting-point for what is to follow, but as furnishing a clue to the play's theme or particular complexion and to the nature of the action.[3]

Elizabethan plays were usually written in a mixture of prose and verse, thus serving to distinguish the noble characters from the humble ones. Here, as common people are present, the scene is written in a mixture of both. The carpenter and the cobbler speak in prose and the two tribunes in verse. Usually in such cases the noble characters, when conversing with the humble ones, speak in prose. In this scene that is not the case. Flavius and Marullus speak in poetry throughout the scene.

As shall be seen later on, none of Shakespeare's scenes is irrelevant. Each scene is indispensable, for each is linked to the foregoing and the following scenes. This scene is the very first in the play, so there is no question of its being linked to any foregoing scene. It is, however, linked to the next. In this scene the feast of Lupercalia is mentioned as well as the celebration of Caesar's triumph and in the next we shall see both taking place.

Shakespeare's scenes, if they are long ones, usually fall into two or more divisions. This will be seen when the other scenes are being discussed. This one also, though quite short (75 lines) does fall into two clear-cut divisions. The first section consists of the dialogue with the commoners, up till line 60, and the rest of the scene, from line 61 to 75, makes up the second section. The first section is considerably longer than the second, but usually Shakespeare balances the different parts of a scene in an orderly manner.

This scene, being the first, prepares us for the future by anticipating certain events. The most important of them, of course, is the conspiracy against Caesar. The two tribunes are very much against Caesar, they think that he is being ambitious, thinking that he is superior to others. This prepares the reader for the conspiracy which leads ultimately to murder. Another thing anticipated is the ease with which the populace turns from Brutus to Antony in the Forum scene. Here the Carpenter and the Cobbler and the other go meekly home when the noblemen tell them to do so. The same fickleness and lack of purpose will bring about the ruin of Rome when the crowd will be swayed by Antony:

> The opening of *Julius Caesar* warned us that, among a people so unstable and so easily led this way or that, the enterprise of Brutus is hopeless.[4]

The scene also offers a glimpse at the manner in which Shakespeare deviated from his sources in order to make his plays dramatically more effective. Caesar's Spanish triumph is dated March 45 B.C. and his celebration of triumph was held in October the same year. The feast of Lupercal is a festival held in honour of the pastoral god Lupercus, held on 15th

February. Shakespeare has brought the two together for the sake of dramatic effect.

Act I, sc. ii

This is the second longest scene of the play, containing 319 lines. In it, we see the feast of Lupercal and Caesar's triumph both taking place. Caesar enters, surrounded by many of the noblemen of Rome and a great crowd.

One of the rituals of this festival is that young men run through the city, striking people with leather thongs which they carry. It is believed that if barren women are struck thus, they can bear children. Mark Antony will be running and Caesar asks him to the sure to touch Calpurnia, his wife, with the thong so that the curse of barrenness may be lifted from her. Just after he says this, a soothsayer calls out and tells him in a cryptic sentence: "Beware the ides of March"[5] Caesar does not give him any importance:

> He is a dreamer. Let us leave him. Pass.[6]

Then everyone goes out except Brutus and Cassius. Now comes the scene in which the latter persuades the former to join the conspiracy against Caesar. Cassius begins by praising Brutus's nobility. While he is still talking, shouting is heard. Brutus guesses rightly that the people have chosen Caesar as their king. Cassius infers from the manner of his speech that Brutus does not want Caesar to be the king. Brutus acknowledges this and urges Cassius to continue whatever he was saying.

Cassius goes about his purpose in a roundabout way. He tells Brutus an anecdote about Caesar and himself. Once on a stormy day Caesar had challenged him to swim across the Tiber. Both of them jumped into the river. But before they could reach their goal Caesar cried out for help. Cassius then jumped into the tumultuous waters and rescued him. This proves that Caesar is but an ordinary man, physically weaker than many, definitely weaker than Cassius. Yet this is the man who has become mighty and godlike now. He tells Brutus how when once Caesar was suffering from fever he shivered and groaned. That is to say, Caesar is subject to human weakness just like any other man.

While he is saying this another shout is heard, signifying as Brutus thinks, some new honour given to Caesar. Cassius goes on with his speech. He now voices his objection to the sudden elevation of Caesar even more clearly:

> Why, man, he doth bestride the narrow world
> Like a Colossus, and we, petty men
> Walk under his huge legs, and peep about
> To find ourselves dishonourable graves.[7]

This is the voice of envy and mortification. Two lines later he speaks two of the best-known and most oft-quoted lines in Shakespeare:

> The fault, Dear Brutus, is not in our stars
> But in ourselves, that we are underlings.[8]

He blames himself and others like himself (Brutus, for example) for not being ambitious enough, energetic enough, to have ascended where Caesar has ascended. He continues the same ideas for some more lines. Brutus promises him that he will think about it all.

At this point Caesar, with his train, enters the stage. There is a short dialogue between him and Antony in which Caesar expresses his liking for fat and jolly men and at the same time it becomes clear that he thinks of himself as superior to others. Speaking of Cassius he says with confidence:

> Such men as he be never at heart's ease
> While they behold a greater than themselves,
> And therefore are they very dangerous.
> I rather tell thee what is to be fear'd
> Than what I fear; for always I am Caesar.[9]

This clearly indicates that he thinks himself to be far superior to his one-time friend Cassius. Then all of them go out except Casca whom Brutus and Cassius detain in order to learn what had been happening all this time.

Casca tells them how Caesar had been offered a crown three times and had refused it every time, but every time with increasing reluctance. Then when he saw that the crowd is cheering him for refusing the crown, he laid his throat bare to them and invited them to cut it. After that he had an epileptic attack, to which he was subject from time to time, and fell down unconscious. Here Cassius interrupts, and, interpreting the word "falling-sickness" differently, says that it was not Caesar who has got the falling-sickness, but the three of them. He means, of course, that they have fallen to the status of being Caesar's humble followers whereas they are actually equal to him, if not better.

All this helps Brutus to partially make up his mind, not only Cassius's attitude and words but other things also. Caesar had worn full regalia at the feast: a purple robe and a golden wreath, and had sat on a golden chair. This was the traditional regalia of the ancient Etruscan kings of Rome. After Casca has gone he tells Cassius that he would like to meet and talk to him the next day and goes away. Cassius, left alone on the stage, delivers a soliloquy which makes it clear that he thinks there is a possibility that Brutus might join pretty soon:

> Well Brutus, thou art noble; yet I see
> Thy honourable mettle may be wrought
> From that it is disposed.[10]

Cassius is by this time quite sure that sooner or later, he will be able to persuade Brutus to join them and the scene ends on this note.

This scene, like the preceding one, is in a mixture of both prose and verse. Casca speaks entirely in prose. He has been portrayed as a rather blunt and unimaginative person who describes everything in a forth-right, prosaic manner. Prose, therefore, is a suitable medium for him. This part of the scene has been studied separately by Herbert Blau who lays special emphasis upon Casca's language. Nothing the fact that the scene between Cassius and Brutus is in verse and the Casca-scene is in prose he points out a significant change has occurred here:

> ...Not only the change in tone, but the character of Casca and, even more important, the reduction in motive, the relaxed intensity of the situation.[11]

The rest of the scene, except for the end, is in blank verse, for Cassius ends the scene with a couplet. This is a common feature in Elizabethan plays—the last lines often come in couplets. Usually these couplets sum up the theme of the scene or the mood of the character who is speaking, or convey, a moral message. The device has been borrowed from Seneca who used such couplets to point out a moral. Shakespeare uses them for other purposes as well, as he has done here. The couplet by Cassius outlines his future course of action and also presages Caesar's fall:

> And after this, let Caesar seat him sure,
> For we will shake him, or worse days endure.[12]

The scene is firmly linked to the foregoing and the ensuing scenes. In sc. i., both the feast of Lupercal and Caesar's triumph had been mentioned and in this one both are presented. It looks forward to the next scene in that Brutus tells Cassius about their next meeting in immediate future and Cassius expresses the hope of including him in the conspiracy. Thus with the second scene of the play, interlinking has already started.

As has been remarked, this scene is the second longest in the play, containing 319 lines. It is divisible into four parts:

I—Line 1... Line 24 (He is a dreamer)—24 Lines

II—L. 25 (Cassius: Will you ...) to L. 175 (of fire...)
no. of Lines—150

III—L. 176 (Brutus: The games...) to
L. 211 (Cae: And tell me...)—no. of Lines—35

IV—L. 212 (Cas.: You pulled...) to the end—Lines 110.

As can be seen from this, the first and the third parts are much shorter than the second and the fourth. Both of the short parts are concerned with Caesar and the two longer ones with Cassius and Brutus. In other words the main business of the scene is the persuading of Brutus by Cassius since it takes up 260 lines out of a total of 319.

The scene expounds for us, not only Caesar's character (his arrogance), but Cassius's (his envy) and Brutus's (his inherent nobility) also. It is a highly functional scene and a very carefully constructed one. It also introduces two major characters, Julius Caesar and Mark Antony, also Calpurnia, Portia and several other minor characters. Of the two female characters, Calpurnia speaks two words and Portia none at all, but they are present on the stage.

Act I, sc. iii

This scene takes place in stormy weather. It opens with a dialogue between Cicero and Casca which is chiefly remarkable for the list of the supernatural portents that Casca gives. First of all this storm is far stronger than any he had seen before and besides it drops fire. Then he saw a slave whose hand burned like twenty torches, yet the hand was not hurt. He mentions several more such omens (*vide* Certain Elizabethan Features, *infra*). All these signs are warnings of some disaster or other.

Then Cicero goes away and Cassius enters to whom Casca unburdens himself. Both of them think that the omens point at Caesar, for he will be meeting the senators the next day and will be given the status of a king. Cassius does not blame Caesar so much as the Romans, for they themselves are bowing down and proclaiming him king over themselves.

Then Cinna the conspirator, comes and Cassius gives him some papers to be put in such places where Brutus will find them. These papers contain messages which will persuade Brutus to join them. He has already decided to do this in the previous scene (Act I, sc. ii, lines 312-16, 323-24). They decide to meet in the portico of the theatre built by Pompey and the scene comes to an end.

This scene is entirely in verse. Casca who spoke prose in the previous scene speaks in verse here. The awe-inspiring omens described require verse in order to be fully effective. The scene looks back to the previous one in that Cassius had mentioned he will put some papers containing certain messages in Brutus's house to persuade him to join the conspirators, and those are the papers given to Cinna in this scene. It looks forward to the next scene because here Cassius is expressing the hope that Brutus will join them and in the next scene

Brutus really does so. Moreover, in that scene we shall see him receiving one of the papers scattered about his house bearing messages. This has been mentioned by Plutarch:

> ...in the night did cast sundrie papers into the Praetor's seate wherein he gave audience and the most of them to this effect: Thou sleepest Brutus, and art not Brutus in deede.[13]

The scene is important in two ways. The first of them is the storm and the omens which together presage disaster. Cassius interprets them thus:

> You shall find
> That heaven hath infus'd them with these spirits
> To make them instruments of fear and warning
> Unto some monstrous state.[14]

He means the condition of Rome which will now be under monarchy. A few lines later he specifically refers to Caesar making the storm a symbol:

> He reads the tempest as a symbol of Caesar's rule, a sign of the overthrow of normal order in society which tyranny implies.[15]

The omens and the storm thus create the proper atmosphere for the impending assassination and waken superstitious awe in the characters. The second function of the scene is to take the action a step forward by distributing the pieces of papers bearing messages in Brutus's house.

This is the last scene of this Act and as such, a definitive one. The first Act is usually one in which the main characters are introduced and the action begun. This is exactly what happens in this one. All the main characters have been introduced in it—actually they are all introduced in the second scene. Some minor ones are still to come, the most important of them being Portia. The action has already begun as Caesar's attitude has alienated the conspirators.

Act II, sc. i

This is the longest scene in the play, containing 334 lines. It opens with Brutus in his orchard on the eve of the Ides of

March. He is meditating over the conspiracy to kill Caesar. In the beginning there are a few lines of dialogue with his servant Lucius. Then comes the famous soliloquy in which he decides upon Caesar's death:

> It must be by his death: and for my part
> I know no personal cause to spurn at him,
> But for the general.[16]

He brings this part of the soliloquy to a close by likening Caesar to a serpent's egg which has to be destroyed before it hatches:

> And therefore think him as a serpent's egg,
> Which, hatch'd, would as his kind, grow mischievous,
> And kill him in the shell.[17]

This soliloquy has been much commented upon (*vide* Ch. 7, Brutus's character, and Ch. 9, soliloquy, *infra*). Here it has to be noted that Brutus has already taken the decision to join the conspiracy and kill Caesar.

Then Lucius brings him one of the messages that have been strewn in his house. It is a brief one, instigating him to bring the possible dictatorship of Caesar to an end. It fires Brutus's patriotism and he also confirms that, of late, he has been receiving such messages quite often. Then Cassius comes, accompanied by five other conspirators, according to appointment.

After conferring together for some time, Brutus and Cassius decide to kill Caesar on the next day when he will come to meet the Senate. It is noticeable that this is not clearly mentioned anywhere. Brutus's influence over the others can be easily judged when, just because he says so, Cicero is excluded from the group though the others are in favour of taking him. Again, just as easily, he spares Antony. Cassius is in favour of killing him as well as Caesar, but as soon as Brutus vetoes the idea they agree with him. This is a clear indication of the great importance they give him and the respect in which they hold him. As will be seen later, this is a wrong decision.

They then wonder if Caesar will come to the Capitol or not, for the day which is drawing is the Ides of March against which Caesar had been already warned. Cassius says that Caesar is superstitious, it is doubtful whether he will come or not. Then Decius takes the responsibility of bringing him to the Senate on the morrow. The conspirators leave.

The scene, however, does not end here, for Portia comes in. There are two domestic scenes in the play and this is the first of them. There are two female characters in it, Calpurnia and Portia and each of them has a domestic scene with her husband. Portia is shown as the ideal helpmate for Brutus, as noble and as unselfish as he himself is. He has concealed the matter of the conspiracy from her because he wants to spare her the worry she would experience otherwise. His motives are entirely unselfish and loving ones. Portia has been drawn as a wife fully worthy of him. What is more, Brutus is also quite aware of this fact.

She has been much perturbed by the fact that Brutus has not slept at night and it is already the beginning of the dawn of the next day. She pleads with him to confide in her, for she can make out that he is intensely troubled in spirit and is also alarmed by the fact that a whole group of men, with their faces hidden, has come to meet him. Brutus tries to fend her off by saying he is ailing, but Portia does not believe him. Finally Brutus agrees to tell her what is troubling him but before he can do so, just at that moment Ligarius comes. He is Brutus's friend and it had been decided that he is to be included among the conspirators. He had been sent for and he has come. Brutus tells him he will tell him everything on the way to the Capitol and the scene ends.

The scene takes in the evening and the night before the Ides of March. It starts in the evening and goes on till the dawn. It is a fateful night when Brutus and the conspirators decide to kill Caesar on the morrow, that is, the Ides or the fifteenth of March, as the Senate is going to honour him with the crown. He will be killed before he can become the king.

The theme of the scene is very serious and the persons involved, except for the servant-boy Lucius, are all noblemen. So the scene is entirely in poetry. Lucius, though he is a servant and speaks very little (usually one line or half of one) speaks in verse as becomes clear in the longest passage he has, which is of four lines. No couplets are used in the scene, not even a Senecan couplet at the end of the scene.

The scene is one of the important scenes of the play and is integrally related to the other scenes. It looks back to the last two scenes in that, in both of them, the conspiracy had been talked about and in this scene everything reaches a climax, and a culmination. The conspirators have a meeting and Brutus joins them. It is linked to the next scene in that, in this one the murder of Caesar is planned and in the next the plan is executed. The scene, moreover, takes place on the 14th of March and the next scene takes place the next day, the Ides of March—a date that is mentioned several times in the course of the scene.

It is highly functional scene as it takes the action forward in a significant manner. It also introduces several new characters: Portia, Decius, Metellus, Trebonius and Ligarius of these the first two had come on the stage in the previous scene but only as part of Caesar's retinue and had not spoken at all. Here, they speak for the first time. Ligarius comes in at the last moment. Nevertheless, it is in his company that Brutus goes out.

The scene is the longest in the play, containing 334 lines, and can be divided into four parts:

I Line 1 to 85 (Brutus: To hide...) No. of Lines—85

II L. 86 (Cas.: I think...) to L . 233 (Br.: Therefore...)
No. of Lines—148

III L. 233 (Por.: Brutus...) to 304 (Br.: Leave me...)
No. of Lines—77

IV L. 309 (Br.: Lucius...) to end. No. of Lines—25.

As can be seen it is the second section that is the longest, constituting more than half of this long scene. This is the part in which the conspirators talk and is therefore the most important part of the scene. As such it is fitting that it should be the longest. The third part of the scene, however, though comprising only 77 lines, is of unique importance and is known as a domestic scene. It shows a different aspect of

Brutus. He is seen here as a husband and Portia's worthy consort. As has already been mentioned, there are two such domestic scenes in the play and this is the first of them. It has also been called a "buffer scene" by S. Musgrove who points out:

> These scenes serve, mainly, to give the audience time to recover the breath after the excitement of one of the tensest scenes in the play.[18]

This is not the only buffer scene of the play. The others will be pointed out as they occur.

Act II, sc. ii

The scene now shifts to Caesar's house. The weather is very bad and Caesar is rather apprehensive, both because of the weather and because Calpurnia had bad dreams in the night. Three times had she dreamt that Caesar was being killed and had cried out. So Caesar sends for a servant to tell the priests to offer a sacrifice which will help them to forecast the future. It was an ancient Roman custom to prophesy by inspecting the dead body of the animal that had been sacrificed.

Calpurnia then comes and tries to persuade him not to leave the house that day. She tells of ominous portents that foretell disaster. Both of these, Calpurnia's dreams and the unfavourable omens, have been mentioned by Plutarch. Caesar, however, is determined to go. Then the servant comes with the prophecy of the priests who have sent Caesar the message that the omens are not at all favourable and tell him not to go out. This shakes Caesar's resolution and he decides not to go to meet the Senate.

Then Decius comes and Caesar recounts Calpurnia's dreams to him. Decius reinterprets the dreams favourably (*vide* Ch. 9, *infra*, the section on *The Supernatural*). He further adds that the Senate is going to confer the crown upon him, thus making him a monarch. This and the hint that they might think Caesar is afraid once more change his mind and he decides to go out. Then the conspirators enter and after them

Antony. Caesar greets all of them and invites them to have a drink with him before they set out. The scene ends here.

It is not a very long scene, comprising 129 lines and is entirely in verse. All the characters in it are noblemen and so they speak in verse. As in the foregoing scene there are no couplets in it.

The scene is firmly linked to the preceding one in that the conspirators had talked about all of them going together to fetch Caesar at about 8 o'clock and that is what they do in this scene. In fact Brutus points out: "Caesar, 'tis stricken eight" (L. 114). Besides, Decius had said he will persuade Caesar to come out if he showed reluctance and that is exactly what he does just before the others enter. It is linked to the third scene after this because in that one he goes out of his house to address the senators which is the subject of discussion here.

As far as the theme is concerned, the scene falls into two divisions. The first part lasts till the entrance of Decius after L. 56. In this part, Caesar at first declares he will go out and then decides not to. After Decius's entrance the second part of the action starts and continues till the end. In this part Caesar decides to go and proceeds accordingly. The two halves are almost the same length and balance each other very neatly.

Within the first part, however, comes the second domestic scene of the play. Once more, we have an anxious wife talking to her husband. The first such scene occurred within the preceding scene, when Portia tried to persuade Brutus to confide in her. The two scenes are eminently comparable because in both we have an anxious wife pleading with her husband. Comparing the two husbands, S. Musgrove finds Brutus to be a better husband than Caesar:

> He neither treats her as an equal, as Brutus had treated Portia, nor does he comfort her as her fearful nature requires; instead, he speaks in his Olympian mode....
>
> That is, Caesar feels the necessity of acting...even before his wife.[19]

The scene is important in two respects. First of all, it sheds light on Caesar's character. We see him as a husband and also as a man who believes in superstitions and also as being susceptible to flattery. Secondly, it shows him setting forth, surrounded by the conspirators. Thus it prepares us for the assassination as, indeed, Calpurnia's dreams and the other supernatural portents also presage. The scene reveals Calpurnia as an anxious wife. We can say that this scene introduces her as in the former scene (Act I, sc. ii) she had spoken only two words.

Act II, sc. iii

This is a very short scene, comprising only 14 Lines. In it, Artemidorus, a well-wisher of Caesar, decides to warn him against Brutus and the others. He has written out a message on a piece of paper which he decides to put in Caesar's hands as he passes along the street near the Capitol. Each one of the conspirators is named in this warning.

In this short scene, there is only one character, Artemidorus reads out the letter which is in prose and then delivers a six-line passage in blank verse. So this very short scene, within its narrow compass, offers the variety of both prose and verse. The six-line passage itself, again, contains variety, for its last two lines make up a couplet. This much of variety is not found in many long scenes as the preceding ones have shown.

A scene like this will be called by Verity a link-scene or a transitional scene. Musgrove calls it by another name. It is one of his buffer-scenes (*vide* the summary of Act I, sc. ii, *supra*). According to him these buffer-scenes serve the purpose of relieving the tension of the foregoing scene and prepares the audience for the ensuing scene. Besides this, each has its own special function also. This scene, for example, serves the purpose of offering Caesar a chance for escaping:

> ...the Artemidorus scene serves to arouse our hopes, even against our previous knowledge of everything, by showing that Caesar still has a chance if he will only take it.[20]

As a link-scene it serves to link the foregoing with the ensuing scene. It is such a very short scene that there is no call for dividing it into separate parts.

Act II, sc. iv

This again is another link scene or buffer scene. S. Musgrove has also called it "the second Portia scene". This is perfectly justified since Portia is the main speaker here. She is very anxious about what is happening at the Capitol and tells Lucius to go there and see the state of things and report back to her:

> Yes, bring me word, boy, if thy lord look well,
> For he went sickly forth; and take good not
> What Caesar doth, which suitors press to him.[21]

Before Lucius can go, however, the soothsayer who had cautioned Caesar enters. Portia finds out from him that Caesar has not yet gone to the Capitol. He says he will stand on the road along which Caesar will pass, and tell him once more to take care against possible danger. Then he goes away and Portia sends Lucius to the Capitol. With this the scene ends.

This is a link-scene like the foregoing one, and, like the foregoing one, it has been called a buffer-scene. The special purpose this scene serves is to shed light on Portia's character. As Musgrove says:

> ...and the Portia scene to exhibit the true womanliness of Brutus's wife, whom we have hitherto seen only as a dignified and purposeful Lady.[22]

This scene is entirely in verse; even Lucius and the soothsayer speak in blank verse. It can be divided into three short parts, the first part lasting up till the entrance of the soothsayer, the second consisting of the dialogue with the soothsayer and the third continuing the dialogue with Lucius. Neither this scene nor the immediately preceding one takes the action forward in any way. They serve to link the longer, more important scenes together and that is why such scenes are known as link-scenes. In the case of these two, of course, the term buffer-scene adds importance to them.

Act III, sc. i

This is the famous assassination scene, occurring nearly in the middle of the play. As the murder occurs in the middle of the play, Emma Smith's observation seems to be especially apt:

> At the play's formal and thematic height is a corpse—the dead Caesar—on stage for some 200 lines in the middle of the play and remains in the minds of the characters throughout.[23]

The scene begins in front of the Capitol, with Caesar being importuned by Artemidorus to read his letter. The first words spoken by Caesar are addressed to the soothsayer:

> Caesar, going into the Senate—house, and speaking merily unto the Soothsayer tolde him the Ides of March be come: so they be, softly answered the Soothsayer, but yet are they not past.[24]

This strikes an ominous note right from the beginning. Then they all go into the senate. The conspirators confer among themselves and send Metellus with a petition to repeal the sentence of banishment on his brother. Caesar refuses him in an offensively arrogant manner. Arrogance, indeed, expressed itself in every word he speaks. Brutus and Cassius support Metellus and plead with Caesar. Again Caesar refuses and speaks of himself in terms which at once brings the word "hybris" to the mind. He likens himself to the polestar in constancy, which sets him apart from everyone else:

> Just as his fall is about to stress the common humanity which binds him to other men, he accentuates unnaturally the distance which separates him from them.[25]

His arrogance is the last straw and the conspirators stab him. Brutus had been kneeling to him, so Caesar's eyes fall on him and he says the famous words "Et tu, Brute" and dies then and there.

Then the other senators are frightened and Brutus pacifies them by making it clear that Caesar will be the only one to be killed. There is general alarm everywhere. Antony has run back to his house. The conspirators are the only ones surrounding Caesar's body. Then comes the famous blood-bath. Brutus says that each one of them should bathe his hands up to the elbows and smear their swords in Caesar's blood and then go to the market-place to proclaim the fall of tyranny: "Let's all cry,

"Peace, freedom and Liberty".[26] Thus bloodshed is converted into a ritual which glorifies it. This is a feature approved by ancient religious custom:

> So in Aeschylus we read that the seven Captains who came against Thebes sacrificed a bull, and dipped their hands in the gore.[27]

They all do as Brutus says, and then Cassius says some highly significant lines:

> How many ages hence
> Shall this our lofty scene be acted over,
> In states unborn, and accents yet unknown![28]

Like almost every line of this scene, these lines have also been much commented upon, particularly because of their association with the stage and their prophetic manner:

(1) In this anticipation of theatrical performance, the play shows an awareness of its own presence and future mythologizing.[29]

(2) This passage belongs to that most traditional class of play images.... It serves, pre-eminently, to glorify the stage.[30]

This blood-bath has not been mentioned by Plutarch or any other ancient writer. It has been invented by Shakespeare. Leo Kirschbaum has suggested five reasons for it:

(1) Shakespeare introduces a scene which in its novelty and brutality excites the spectators and grasps their attention.

(2) He underscores the fact that the conspirators are blood-thirsty men.

(3) It comes as a shock.

(4) The conspiracy openly degenerates.

(5) The blood of Caesar begins to spread.[31]

They have barely finished the ritual when Antony's servant comes. He brings the message from Antony that he is ready to come and follow Brutus if Brutus in his turn will tell him it is safe to come. Brutus gives the assurance and Antony comes. He is not antagonistic to the conspirators and tells them to kill him if they want to. Brutus tells him that they do not want to kill anybody else and will explain to him "why I, that did love Caesar while I struck him". Antony then shakes the bloody hand of each conspirator and tells them that he wants to deliver the funeral oration. Brutus agrees at once. Cassius, having more practical sense, advises Brutus not to allow him to speak. Brutus then puts three conditions to Antony: (1) he will not blame the conspirators, (2) he shall praise Caesar and say that he, Antony, has the conspirator's permission to speak, and (3) he shall speak from the same pulpit after Brutus himself has spoken. This is the second fatal mistake made by Brutus. The first was when he did not agree to kill Antony in the conspiracy scene, and the second lies in granting him permission to speak at all, under whatever conditions it might be.

After this, the conspirators leave and Antony is alone on the stage. Now the audience realizes that he had only pretended to be friendly with the conspirators, his loyalty is still with Caesar. He had not really betrayed Caesar. In fact, nothing is farther from his intentions. He now pronounces a terrible curse:

> Woe to the hand that shed this costly blood!
> Over thy wounds now do I prophesy
> . . .   .
> A curse shall light upon the limbs of men;
> Domestic fury and fierce civil strife
> Shall cumber all the parts of Italy.[32]

The soliloquy continues for some more lines and then Octavius's servant comes and tells him that Octavius would nearly reach Rome by nightfall. Caesar had written to him to come and he is coming. Antony tells the servant to wait till he had delivered his funeral oration and then go to Octavius and tell him everything, including the Roman citizen's reactions to his own speech. This will mean that Antony has already decided in his mind to inflame the mob against the conspirators. The scene ends.

It is the most important scene of the play, though it is not the longest. It contains less than 297 lines while there are three scenes in the play of more than 300 lines. Nor is it the central scene, for the play is in eighteen scenes and this one is the eighth. That is, it is nearly in the middle of the play, but not exactly. It is entirely in poetry. There is little doubt, however, that it is the climactic scene. Some critics would, however, give that honour to the next scene, in which both Brutus and Antony speak at the Forum. It must be kept in the mind that all these scene divisions are given by the editor, not by the author, for Elizabethan plays were written in one continuous stream and scene divisions were introduced later, so the position of the central scene too is doubtful.

All the foregoing scenes lead up to this and this scene influences all the ensuing ones. Instead of saying that this scene is linked to the others, it will be more appropriate to stay that all the other scenes of the play are linked to it.

The dialogue with Octavius's servant has been designated as a buffer-scene by Musgrove. He ascribes three functions to this short dialogue or scene-within-scene. It acts as a buffer, serving to bring a moment of relaxation between two scenes of great tension—the murder scene and the Forum scene. Secondly it takes the action forward by mentioning the coming of Octavius, which implies that Octavius is ready to seize power. The third reason is purely a matter of stagecraft, for it gives Antony someone to help him carry Caesar's body to the Forum. By bringing in Octavius's servant Shakespeare has thus, very economically, combined the second and the third functions in an admirable manner.

Act III, sc. ii

This is the famous Forum scene. As had been agreed in the previous scene, Brutus is the first to deliver his funeral oration. Some of the people are led off by Cassius to listen to him and some remain behind to listen to Brutus. It is a speech of ideal oratory.

Brutus's oration is in prose. It is one of the most famous passages in the whole of Shakespeare. He is an intellectual and his speech appeals, not to the emotion but to the intellect of the people. It is a speech in the classical manner, every sentence carefully constructed and balanced. But it is a cold, intellectual speech. He speaks of honour throughout the speech and appeals to their sense of honour, justice and patriotism:

> Believe me for mine honour, and have respect to mine honour that you may believe.... Not that I loved Caesar less, but that I loved Rome more.... As Caesar loved me, I weep for him, as he was fortunate, I rejoice at it; as he was valiant, I honour him; but as he was ambitious, I slew him.[33]

The speech appeals to the populace and they are vociferous in their appreciation. They suggest that his statue should be erected and that instead of Caesar, he may be crowned.

This is highly ironical, for it is to prevent monarchy that they had killed Caesar. It also hints at the fact that the mob does not much care whether they have monarchy or dictatorship. Politically, they are not very conscious.

After Brutus, it is the turn of Antony. From the very beginning his appeal is to the feelings and emotions of the audience. He keeps strictly faithful to the three conditions imposed upon him by Brutus. One of them was that he should speak after Brutus and he is doing that. Another was that he should say that he was delivering the speech with their permission and that is the first line he says: "For Brutus's sake I am beholding to you". The third condition was that he should not blame the conspirators. He around this clause very cleverly, by repeating again and again that Brutus is an honourable man. This has become the classic example of irony. Gradually the attitude of the crowd sways away from the conspirators to Caesar's favour. He gets shows them Caesar's wounds. By this time, as a result of his eloquence, the crowd is already enraged. Then he reads them Caesar's will in which he has left 75 drachmas to every citizen. Then he has left all his property on that side of the Tiber, containing gardens and orchards, to the citizens of Rome as public pleasure grounds.

By this time, the crowd has turned completely against the conspirators. They cry that they will seek out the conspirators and kill them, but before that they cremate the body of Caesar.

Plutarch gives a vivid account of how the mob tore down benches, etc. to get wood, how the veteran soldiers of Caesar's army put their wreaths on the funeral pyre.

This is exactly what Antony had wanted. Now he does not have to do anything. While he stands and contemplates the anger of the mob, Octavius' servant comes and tells him that Octavius has already reached Rome. The servant also tells him that Brutus and Cassius have fled the city. Antony goes off to meet Octavius and Lepidus at Caesar's house and the scene ends.

This scene is almost at the centre of the play. As has been pointed out, the play has eighteen scenes in all, and this is the ninth. This and the next scene are the two central scenes but as the next scene is not an important one, this can be regarded as the central scene. Both prose and poetry have been used in it because Brutus's wonderful speech is in prose. It is in extremely well-written prose, every sentence is constructed with classical economy and polish. But as the play shows it is not such an effective speech as Antony's, which appeals to the emotions of the mob.

This is a key-scene of the play for it is from here onward, the action takes a different turn. It harks back to the murder-scene, for in that the matter of the funeral oration had been decided. It looks forward to the immediately following scene in the depiction of mob violence and to the scene after that because here Antony talks of going to meet Octavius and Lepidus and this meeting takes place in that scene.

The scene falls into two neat divisions, the first concerned with Brutus's speech and the second with Antony's. The second is far longer than the first, as the first is of 63 lines and the second of 200 lines, not counting the dialogue with Octavius's servant.

Both of the funeral speeches have been analysed in great detail, particularly that of Antony. There are different stages in his oration and the display of Caesar's dead body is a particularly effective move:

> It is, indeed, now a religious relic that is being displayed to call for its own intensity of responding feelings.[34]

Antony, indeed, shows himself a master orator while disclaiming all pretensions to oratory. He rouses the mob to fury:

> The speech of Antony, with its mastery of every phase of feeling, is a perfect sonata upon the instruments of the human emotions.[35]

The scene, moreover, shows the fickleness of the Romans who are swayed once by Brutus and then again by Antony. This biddable, persuadable quality has been amply shown in the first scene of the play, when the two Tribunes upbraided the men for wanting to celebrate Caesar's victory and instead of celebrating they all meekly went back. Antony knows their nature and fully exploits it, to his own advantage.

Act III, sc. iii

This is a short scene, comprising only 38 lines. It shows the destructive violence which Antony's speech has unleashed in Rome. The enraged populace is seeking its victims and they find Cinna the poet. There is another person named Cinna who is one of the conspirators and the mob knows about him. So they vent their anger on the poet just because he has the same name, a coincidence:

> The sinister little episode (Act III, sc. iii) of the destruction of Cinna the poet for a chance coincidence of name, comes effectively to announce the brutality which will from now on so frequently preside over the course of events.[36]

This can be regarded as a link-scene that links the third and the fourth Acts together. It is the last scene of the third Act. It does not take the action forward, but it amply illustrates the kind of irrational carnage that will take place as a result of the assassination of Caesar which was done with high and noble visions in mind.

With the third Act, one phase of the action is over. Caesar's murder, to which the play had been gradually building up, has been accomplished. There is still the battle at

Philippi to bring the play to a conclusion, but many critics have remarked upon the anticlimactic nature of the next two Acts. One has the feeling that the main business of the play is over and whatever comes next will be in the nature of an anticlimax. This is mainly because Julius Caesar, who gives his name to the play and should have the status of the hero is dead. According to stage conventions and the rules of tragedy this would imply the end of the play. Actually however, from the structural point of view, only half of the action is over. The play will go on to show the tragic end of Brutus who also gains the status of the hero of this play.

Act IV, sc. i

This scene shows the three persons who will make up the Triumvirate and will rule Caesar's empire, gathered together in Antony's house and planning out their future course of action. They are preparing, in cold blood, a list of the men whom they are condemning to death. Among them are close relatives of the three men themselves—Lepidus's brother and Antony's nephew. Lepidus's brother later escaped and Antony actually had no nephew. It has been suggested hy T.S. Dorsch that Shakespeare has brought in this non-existent nephew for two reasons: to show the cold-blooded quality of Antony's character, and to

> ...bring about a contrast with Brutus's refusal to take the precaution of killing Antony himself, which was essential for the success of the conspiracy.[37]

Then Lepidus goes off to bring Caesar's will. When he is gone, Antony's shrewdness as a politician comes to the fore. Neither Octavius nor he likes the idea of giving Lepidus a third of Caesar's kingdom, but they mean to make use of him as a scapegoat and a tool:

> To ease ourselves of diverse sland'rous loads,
> He shall but bear them as the ass bears gold,
> To groan and sweat under the business,
> Either led or driven, as we point the way;
> And having brought our treasures where we will,
> Then take we down his load, and turn him off.[38]

This shows the utterly selfish and conscienceless nature of Antony. Octavius is reluctant, but Antony persuades him quite easily. The entire business is a sordid one:

> The first scene (Act IV, sc. i) reflects the political spirit which, in one form or another, will from this time forth dominate the action.... The last words of the scene, spoken by Octavius, stress the insecurity that surrounds the entire political future.[39]

The scene, thus, sets the tone of the ones to follow, and highlights the opportunism and dishonesty on which the rule of the triumvirate is going to be based.

The scene is entirely in verse, which is fitting as all the characters are noble ones, and the subject is the founding of the Roman empire. It can be divided into two unequal parts. The first part consists of the conversation till the exit of Lepidus (Line 11) and the rest of the scene (40 Lines) makes up the second part. It is the second part which contains the discussion on Lepidus and is consequently much longer than the first.

The scene takes the action forward by showing the future Triumvirate already at work. The battle is not even mentioned. Yet it is linked to the third scene, in which Antony and Octavius are mentioned many times. This scene, as a matter of fact, serves as an introduction to Act IV just as the foregoing scene served as a conclusion to Act III.

Act IV, sc. ii

In this scene, the attention shifts to Brutus and his followers and the locale from Rome to Sardis. Brutus has three of his friends (except Cassius) with him and their army. Lucillus had gone to meet Cassius and has brought back messages from him. It appears from what he tells Brutus that Cassius has, for some reason, become angry with Brutus.

They have hardly talked this much when Cassius himself comes with his army. He accuses Brutus of having done wrong with him. Brutus realizes that they should talk in privacy and both of them withdraw into their tent and the brief scene ends here.

It is a short scene (52 lines) written entirely in verse. Though short, it falls into two neat, almost equal divisions. The first part consists of 29 lines, lasts till the arrival of Cassius and the second part consists of 27 lines. It is integrally related to the next scene as it foreshadows the famous quarrelling scene between Brutus and Cassius which will take place in it. This is thus a link-scene or a transitional scene which is important, not in itself, but in so far as it takes the play onward from one scene into another without there being any sense of discontinuity or abruptness.

All these remarks would apply when this scene and the next are considered as independent ones. Actually, however, in the Folio the second and the third scenes are merged into one. It is for the convenience of the reader that T.S. Dorsch the editor of the Arden edition, has divided the scene into two parts.

Act IV, sc. iii

This is an extremely important scene with two important events occurring in it: the quarrel and the reconciliation between Brutus and Cassius, and the appearance of the Ghost of Caesar.

Cassius starts the scene by accusing Brutus of condemning Lucius Pella of having taken bribes and then disregarding Cassius own letter in this man's favour. Brutus in turn accuses him of having "an itching palm". Mutual recriminations pile up till they are quarrelling like children. It is given very credibly:

Brutus: Go to! you are not, Cassius.
Cass: I am.
Br.: I say you are not.
Cass.: Urge me no more. I shall forget myself.[40]

This childish exchange continues. A few lines later, they again talk like children:

Br.: You durst not so have tempted him.
Cass.: I durst not?
Brutus: No.
Cass.: What? durst not tempt him?
Br.: For your life you durst not.[41]

By this time both of them have realized that a serious quarrel, followed by their deserting each other at this juncture, will bring disaster. So both of them cool down and become reasonable and finally get reconciled:

> The healing of this breach and the return to at least the appearance of unity are accomplished with no small tact. The conspirators, seeing the abyss opening at their feet, draw back in horror.[42]

While they are in a mood to be reconciled, an interruption comes in the shape of a poet who enters by force and exhorts them not to quarrel. After he is gone Brutus sends for wine and calls the generals for a meeting. It is at this time that Brutus tells Cassius that Portia is dead.

Cassius is overcome with shame and remorse at having quarrelled with Brutus while he is in this grief-struck condition, and the reconciliation between them is complete. Then they drink and Titinius and Messala enter. They hold responsible posts in the army. Brutus tells them that they have received information that Octavius and Antony have gathered together an army and are coming rowards Philippi which is very near their own camp. Messala gives them more news, that the three of them have put a hundred senators to death, Cicero being one of them.

Then follows a curious passage. Messala asks Brutus if he has received any news about his wife and he says that he has not. This is asked twice and both the times Brutus returns a negative answer. Then Messala tells him that Portia is dead. The reader knows that Brutus knows this. Why he pretends not to know is a mystery and much has been written on "The Duplicate Revelation of Portia's Death". An explanation is that when Messala asks him the question Brutus perhaps thinks that the news he had received was a false one:

> I hold that Brutus most firmly established his right to be considered an able general at the moment when the hope that Portia may be alive...is snuffed out.[43]

He reacts to this news (to which he has already become accustomed) with typical stoic dignity and the plans for the battle proceed. They decide to march to Philippi. At first Cassius demurs, but Brutus puts forward valid reasons and it is decided that they will start the next day.

Brutus now prepares to retire for the night. He calls two more of his attendants, Varro and Claudius, to share his tent with him. He asks Lucius to sing a song who falls asleep even while singing. Brutus however cannot sleep and thinks of reading. It is at this point that the Ghost comes. At first Brutus thinks it to be a hallucination and pours forth questions:

> Br.: Art thou any thing?
> Art thou some god, some angel or some devil,
> That makes my blood cold and my hair to stare?
> Speak to me what thou art.
>
> Ghost: Thy evil spirit, Brutus.[44]

It tells him that it will meet him again at Philippi and as soon as Brutus affirms this, it vanishes. Brutus then asks Lucius, Varro and Claudius whether they had seen anything. All say they had not, though, as Brutus tells them, they had cried out in their sleep. The scene ends with Brutus sending a message to Cassius to set out first in the morning to be followed by Brutus.

The scene is entirely in poetry. This is appropriate because not only are the characters noble ones, but the theme too is very serious. There are three subjects treated in this scene: the quarrel and the reconciliation, the plans for battle and the Ghost of Caesar. All three are serious subjects. A little variety has been provided in the versification: there is a couplet by the poet who enters forcibly. He speaks a total of seven lines, but of these two make up a couplet. This is the only variety provided in versification, so slight as to be negligible.

The scene is firmly linked to the rest of the play. It comes immediately after the preceding scene in point of time and the subject, that is, the quarrel, has been already foreshadowed in that scene. It is linked to the later scenes in that the plans for the battle, which will form the main subject of Act V, is partially chalked out here. The Ghost also prepares us for the battle, by mentioning that it will meet Brutus at Philippi.

It can be roughly divided into three parts. The first part lasts till the entrance of the poet after l. 122. The second part commences with line 123 and continues up till line 234 when Lucius enters with Brutus's gown. The third part commences here and continues till the end. The three subjects pointed out above are treated in these three parts.

The first part is concerned with the quarrel between the two friends. It would seem to be a pointless incident, as the quarrel is made up and does not affect anyone. Shakespeare has actually followed Plutarch very closely here. Plutarch in his *Life of Brutus* tells how they went into a room and closed the door:

> Then they began to pour out their complaints one to the other, and grew hot and lowde, earnestly accusing each other, and at length both fell a weeping.[45]

Besides being historically true, it provides human interest and dramatic suspense, so Shakespeare did not omit the incident. Dryden compares this scene with one by Euripides and another by Fletcher and remarks:

> The occasion...is the same, grounded upon friendship; and the quarrelling of two virtuous men, raised by natural degrees to the extremity of passion, is concluded in all three to the declination of the same passion and concluded with a warm renewing of their friendship.[46]

Shakespearean critics have analysed the quarrel stage by stage.

The second part of the scene begins with the interruption occasioned by the Poet (*vide* Chapt. 7, *infra* for more information on this head) and comprises the full reconciliation of the friends and the plans about the battle. There are, thus, three sub-sections within it.

The third part comprises the entrance of the Ghost (*vide* Chap. 9, *infra* for more information). Not only does this afford the element of Spectacle or *opsis* as required by Aristotle, it also confirms Brutus that a decisive battle will be fought at Philippi. This is the only appearance of the Ghost, for though it says it will meet Brutus at Philippi and though Brutus himself talks about it later, this second appearance is not shown on the stage. All in all, the scene presents a great variety of events and of dramatic tension.

Act V, sc. i

The scene has now shifted to Philippi and to the camp of Antony. They have come to know that Brutus's army is coming down from the hills to the plains of Philippi. Even as they are talking Brutus enters with the others to have a parley. All that happens is that they accuse each other and no talks about peace are held. Battle is to be joined.

Then Octavius and Antony leave. Brutus and Lucius draw apart to talk and Cassius talks to Messala. He says that this day is his birthday and talks of ominous signs that foretell their defeat at the battle. He and Brutus then talk as if they might not meet again and bid each other farewell. This is what will really happen, for they will not meet again.

This scene, written entirely in verse, takes the action forward in a decisive manner. The two armies face each other for the first time and prepare to give battle. It can be divided into three short parts. The first part is concerned with Octavius and Antony, till line 20. The second part commences with the entrance of Brutus and is concerned with the talk of the two leaders. It lasts till line 66 when Octavius and the others leave. Then, line 66 onwards till the end is the third part and is concerned with Brutus's group. The first and the third parts, thus, parallel each other. Both are concerned with the conversations among the leaders of the two armies. The middle section is concerned with the two groups together. It is thus a well-constructed scene.

The scene is linked to the preceding and the ensuing scenes because just now all the scenes are concerned with the fateful battle. Caesar's Ghost, also, had mentioned the battle of Philippi and this takes place on the eve of it.

Act V, sc. ii

This is the shortest scene in the play, containing only 6 lines. It consists of a single passage by Brutus addressed to Messala. He sends Messala to call the legions on the other side to come forth and charge. It generates the hope that his army may win the battle. It is a link scene between sc. i and sc. iii.

Act V, sc. iii

Brutus's soldiers are running away. Cassius is trying to hold them back without success. While he and Titinius are talking Pindarus, who is Cassius's servant, comes in and tells them to go further away. Cassius's tents have been set on fire by Antony. Titinius goes to the battlefield and Pindarus can see him taken prisoner and tells Cassius so. Seeing that there is no hope of winning, Cassius then sets Pindarus free (he had been Cassius's slave) and with his help kills himself.

Then we have a piece of dramatic irony. Cassius had killed himself on being told that Titinius had been taken prisoner and now Titinius himself enters with Messala. The trend of battle has changed. Now Octavius is being overthrown by Brutus's army while Cassius's army has been defeated by Antony. Titinius and Messala have come to console Cassius with this news and they find his dead body. They realize that Cassius's death is the result of a mistake. Then Messala goes off to meet Brutus and Titinius takes this chance of doing away with himself, because he is Cassius's friend.

Just after this, Brutus, accompanied by others, comes in. He has been told by Messala of Cassius's death and wants to see the dead body. They find not only Cassius's, but Titinius's dead body as well. There is no time to mourn, for the battle is still raging on and Brutus goes away to flight, with all the pent-up grief in his heart.

This too, like the previous and the ensuing scenes, is a battle-scene. Two of Brutus's friends and his mainstay Cassius die in it. It is an eventful and dynamic scene, full of turns and twists that take the reader by surprise. Cassius dies, paradoxically, with the name of Caesar, the man he had helped to kill, on his lips:

> Caesar, thou art reveng'd,
> Even with the sword that killed thee.[47]

Act V, sc. iv

This is another battle-scene and has for its main event the surrender of Lucilius who, in order to save Brutus, pretends to be him and the soldiers, not knowing him, take him as prisoner. Then Antony comes in and recognizes him. He directs the soldiers to treat him with all honour. It is a link-scene, or transitional scene.

Act V, sc. v

This is the last scene of this tumultuous Act and of the play as well. It opens with Brutus surrounded by his followers. He asks Clitus first to kill him as now there is no hope of winning the battle and he does not want to be taken prisoner by Antony. Clitus refuses and so does Dardanius whom Brutus asks next. Then he calls Volumnius and tells him that the Ghost of Caesar has appeared twice to him, once as Sardis (which has already been shown on the stage in Act IV, sc. iii) and once last night at Philippi, as it had promised. He requests Volumnius to kill him, but Volumnius also refuses. Then Brutus tells each of them, except Strato, to go away. He addresses them in moving words:

> My heart doth joy that yet in all my life
> I found no man but he was true to me.[48]

These are noble sentiments by any standard, yet T.S. Eliot has spoken detrimentally of them, that Brutus is cheering himself up. The words, however, have not been put into Brutus's mouth by Shakespeare. Brutus had really said something, meaning what he means here, as has been given by Plutarch (*vide* Chap. 7, *infra*, Brutus's character).

After they go away, he tells Strato to hold his sword in such a manner that he will be able to fall upon it and kill himself. He too, like Cassius, dies with Caesar's name on his lips:

> Caesar, now be still;
> I kill'd thee not with half so good a will.[49]

Then Antony, Octavius and many others enter and Antony speaks the famous epilogue on Brutus:

> This was the noblest Roman of them all
> . . . .
> His life was gentle, and the elements
> So mix'd in him, that Nature might stand up
> "And say to all the world, "This was a man"![50]

The last words of the play are spoken by Octavius. He declares the battle to be at end, and brings the play to a close with a couplet:

> So call the field to rest, and let's away,
> To part the glories of this happy day.[51]

This scene is a fitting one for a tragedy, showing as it does the glorious and noble death of Brutus. It is true that he commits suicide which is an unforgiveable sin according to Christianity. But it is not a mortal sin according to Roman custom. It was, on the contrary, an honorable and dignified death, for Brutus chose death to the dishonor of being taken prisoner. Like most of the incidents in the play the story of Brutus's death as given by Plutarch has been closely followed by Shakespeare. The play belongs as much to Brutus as to Caesar, who is the titular hero. It is, therefore, designated as a Roman tragedy not a Roman history play.

The play does not contain a separate Epilogue, so the speech of Octavius is considered to be in the nature of an epilogue.

NOTES

1. Ure, *op. cit.*, p. 138.
2. Act I, sc. i, ll. 72-75, pp. 7-8.
3. Ure, *op. cit.*, p. 198.
4. Bradley, *op. cit.*, p. 45.
5. Act I, sc. ii, ll. 18, 23, p. 9.
6. Act I, sc. ii, l. 24, p. 9.
7. Act I, sc. ii, ll. 133-36, p. 15.
8. Act I, sc. ii, ll. 138-39, pp. 15-16.
9. Act I, sc. ii, ll. 205-09, p. 19.
10. Act I, sc. ii, ll. 305-07, p 23.

11. Ure, *op. cit.*, p. 70.
12. Act I, sc. ii, ll. 318-19, p. 24.
13. Bullough, *op. cit.*, p. 82.
14. Act I, sc.iii, ll. 78-81, p. 27.
15. Derek Traversi, *Shakespeare: The Roman Plays*, London, Hollis & Carter, 1963, p. 31.
16. Act II, sc. i, ll. 10-12, pp. 33-34.
17. Act II, sc. i, ll. 32-34, p. 35.
18. Ure, *op. cit.*, p. 60.
19. *Ibid.*, p. 59.
20. *Ibid.*, p. 60.
21. Act II, sc. iv, ll. 13-15, p. 59.
22. Ure, *op. cit.,* p. 60.
23. Smith, *op. cit.*, p. 6.
24. Bullogh, *op. cit.*, p. 83, from Plutarrch's *Life of Caesar*.
25. Traversi, *op. cit.*, p. 45.
26. Act III, sc. i, l. 110, p. 69.
27. Ure, *op. cit.*, p. 154.
28. Act III, sc. i, ll. 111-13, p. 69.
29. Emma Smith, *op. cit.*, p. 7.
30. Ure, *op. cit.*, p. 29.
31. *Ibid.*, p. 157.
32. Act III, sc. i, ll. 258-64, p. 76.
33. Act III. Sc. ii, ll. 14-27, pp. 78-79.
34. Traverse, *op. cit.*, p. 56
35. Ure, *op. cit.*, p. 38.
36. Traversi, *op. cit.*, p. 57.
37. Dorsch, footnote, p. 91 of the text.
38. Act IV, sc. i, ll. 19-25, p. 92.
39. Traversi, *op. cit.*, pp. 58-59.
40. Act IV, sc. iii, ll. 32-35, p. 99.
41. Act IV, sc. iii, ll. 59-62, pp. 100-01.
42. Traversi, *op. cit.*, p. 65.

43. Warren D. Smith, *The Duplicate Revelation of Portia's Death*, quoted in K. Muir, *Shakespeare's Tragedies Sequence*, London, Hutchinson Univ. Library, 1972, p. 51.
44. Act IV, sc. iii, ll. 277-81, pp. 111-12.
45. Bullough, *op. cit.*, p. 114.
46. Ure, *op. cit.*, p. 29.
47. Act V, sc. iii, ll. 45-6, p. 121.
48. Act V, sc. v, ll. 34-5, p. 127.
49. Act V, sc. v, ll. 50-51, p. 128.
50. Act V, sc. v, ll. 68, 74-75, p. 129.
51. Act V, sc. v, ll. 79-80, p. 130.

5
The Major Themes

One of the required elements for excellence is unity. A literary work must have unity in order to pass the test of time. It is necessary for a play to have a definite theme or idea around which it is to be constructed. Shakespeare's plays, however, are so complex that it is difficult to point at a single idea and declare it to be the central theme. *Julius Caesar* is a very straightforward play, yet in its case also there has been great diversity of opinion. Some of these views will be discussed now. The study of a theme central to any play is of comparatively recent date. One of the earliest of Shakespearean critics to perceive a unifying theme was Paul Stapfer at the end of the nineteenth century. His will be the first view to be considered.

(a) The Spirit of Caesarism

This is a very valuable opinion and it explains the spirit of the play as well as the significance of the title. The title is often taken to be a misnomer, as Caesar appears in only three scenes and the play is actually dominated by Brutus. Paul Stapfer, however, argues that it is the spirit of Caesarism that moulds the play:

> It is not the spirit of any one man, but the spirit of a new era about to begin—the spirit of Caesarism—that fills Shakespeare's play and gives it its unity and moral significance and therefore it is that this tragedy, in which Caesar appears in only three scenes, and neither says nor

> does anything of importance, is called *Julius Caesar* and not *Marcus Brutus*.[1]

Thus, he starts to argue from the reactions to the Forum speech of Brutus, the populace cried out for Brutus to be crowned: "Let him be Caesar". That was the mentality at the time. The days of the Republic were passing away, the new era that was going to come would be of imperialism, Caesarism, which Brutus had not been able to perceive. It is the establishment of this spirit that was brought about by the murder of Caesar. The Roman Empire was just being established and the battle at Philippi with its consequent Triumvirate will bring it to full flower, beginning the long line of Roman emperors. It is but fitting, from this point of view, that the play should be named after Caesar. Many critics have tried to justify the title of the play by arguing that though Caesar is present in only three scenes, actually he dominates the play because all the time the other characters are either being motivated by him, or referring to him repeatedly. There is no need, if Stapfer's view is accepted, to justify the title by referring to the character of Caesar. As this critic affirms, it is the spirit of Caesarism that is signified by the title, not the individual character who lives and dies in it.

This view turns the title into a symbol and all the critics may not agree with it. It is a well-known fact that in tragedies the title always refers, not to any symbolic value, but to the person who is the hero of it.

(b) Personal Judgement vs. Politics

L.C. Knights denies the validity of the view given above and lays stress on the personality of characters themselves. According to him Shakespeare has studied this theme repeatedly in his plays. The plays he specifically mentions are *Othello* and *Troilus and Cressida* in which Shakespeare has presented the theme of:

> ...what happens when personal judgement tries to move exclusively on a political plane.[2]

Julius Caesar is a play about historical events and these were political ones. But this does not mean that the stress falls on history and politics all the time, while the personality of the characters is neglected. That is not the case at all. In fact, Shakespeare takes every opportunity to stress the personal aspect of the characters, including their domestic life. He points out Caesar's deafness, his fainting fits, his superstitions, etc. These are entirely personal traits though not a personal trait like his arrogance which brings about his downfall. His domestic life has also been touched. In fact, that is the first characteristic that is presented: his anxiety as a husband for Calpurnia's barrenness (*vide* Chap. 5, *supra*). In the domestic scene before he sets out for the Senate he allows himself to be persuaded by Calpurnia to stay at home and not go out. There is no actual need to stress all these personal traits, but Shakespeare has repeatedly done so. This is because he wants to present Caesar as a person first and a political figure after that.

With Brutus, the tendency to stress the personal aspect is equally strong. His nobility and integrity are publicly known attributes. Shakespeare, in addition, gives the intimate details of his natural daily life. His kindness to his young servant Lucius is a most remarkable feature. When the boy falls asleep in Act II, sc. i, he looks at him affectionately and does not wake him. Again when in Act IV, sc. iii everyone has gone he observes that Lucius is feeling sleepy. When he needs some music he asks Lucius if he can play some music for him, he does not issue an order. His dialogue with Portia is especially noteworthy, for he treats her as an equal and wants to spare her all worries and anxieties. Observing all these factors L.C. Knights says:

> That we are intended to be aware of the characters as men, of the faces behind the masks, is clear enough.[3]

But both of these characters are all the time trying to separate their public actions from their private life. Caesar even talks of himself in the third person. This can be looked upon as the result of arrogance, it can also be taken as an attempt to dissociate his public self and public actions from his private life. The same is the case, though not so openly, with Brutus. His friendship with Caesar is a case in point. We are told, right from the beginning, that he is Caesar's friend, yet he separates this friendship from his policy—the policy that decries dictatorship.

Shakespeare thus shows how the characters ruin themselves and their country by separating their personal life from their public life—a theme that occurs in many plays.

(c) Spiritual Struggle in Brutus

This is a view held by many, in fact the majority of Shakespearean critics. It has been expressed in the most emphatic manner by Virgil K. Whitaker who considers the play as belonging to the tradition of morality plays (*vide* Chap. 4, *supra*). In fact he takes the attitude of those who regard Brutus as the hero of the play to its logical conclusion.

He regards the play as a tragedy of moral choice and the choice is Brutus's. It follows then that this is the main theme of the play. The morality plays present the hero faced with an important choice—the choice between good and evil—which will ultimately either save or damn his soul. *Dr. Faustus* is the best of non-mediaeval plays in this tradition. Shakespeare chose to take up the same problem in *Julius Caesar* and shows the climactic point in this spiritual struggle in Brutus's famous soliloquy in the orchard.

Before that soliloquy, the play had been leading up to it in the sense that the conspirators had been trying their best to enlist the support of Brutus. The long dialogue between Cassius and Brutus in Act I, sc. ii is aimed at achieving this end. In the next scene also the topic is brought up:

Cinna: O Cassius, if you could
But win the noble Brutus to our party—

Cass.: Come, Casca, you and I will ere this day
See Brutus at his house: three parts of him
Is ours already, and the man entire
Upon the next encounter yields him ours.[4]

After this comes the soliloquy in the orchard. Shakespeare has concentrated the whole of this spiritual struggle in this one soliloquy and Whitaker lays special stress on it:

> ...his technique is one of suggestion rather than of complete representation. There was no need for him to portray the entire mental struggle leading up to a crucial choice.[5]

Usually, in a morality play, the act of choosing between good and evil is protracted over many scenes, and within the play the hero undergoes many trials and tribulations related to this choice. Marlowe too presented the choice (like Shakespeare) in one important, long soliloquy, but within the play, after the choice is made he presents many moments of hesitation and conflict. Shakespeare, like Marlowe, presents the act of choice in one soliloquy, but does not present any hesitation or conflict once the choice is made. Instead, he focuses upon the consequences of that choice—the murder, the mob violence, the battle, the defeat, etc.

In this all-important soliloquy, he provides a background of conflict and meditation by implying that Brutus had already been thinking about the choice and decided upon the murder of Caesar. It is as though he starts speaking abruptly, in the middle of his thoughts:

> It must be by his death: and for my part,
> I know no personal cause to spurn at him,
> But for the general.[6]

The tone of these opening lines imply that much thought has gone before it. Thus we have, in the foregoing scene, the attempt to make him face the choice, then we have him making the choice, but after long debates and struggles within himself. Everything in the play up till now is concerned with this choice. The play hinges upon it.

It becomes even more concerned, not less, with the choice once it is made. We have the conspirators coming in and the plans made to kill Caesar. Then there is the actual killing itself. Thereafter we have Brutus's own speech wherein he justifies his choice and his consequent action:

> Not that I loved Caesar less, but that I loved Rome more. Had you rather Caesar were living and die all

> slaves, that Caesar were dead, to live all free men?...but as he was ambitious, I slew him.[7]

Whatever happens after this is, indeed, the result of the choice made by him. He however, unlike Dr. Faustus, does not show any hesitation or conflict within himself after this. He is quite sure in his mind that his choice has been the right one:

> So are we Caesar's friends, that have abridg'd
> His time of fearing death.
>
> . . .   .
>
> As fire drives out fire, so pity pity—
> Hath done this deed on Caesar.
>
> . . .   .
>
> I have done no more to Caesar than you
> Shall do to Brutus.
>
> . . .   .
>
> Did not great Caesar bleed for justice's sake?
> What villain touch'd his body, that did stab
> And not for Justice?[8]

These, and many more examples in the play, prove that subsequent to the choice, Brutus does not regret it. He is sorry for having killed his friend, but not for a would-be king.

The battle at Philippi and its result, all are the consequences of the choice made by Brutus. In fact, that one choice changed the fate of a nation. It is from this point of view that Whitaker calls the play a tragedy of moral choice and consequently moral choice is the theme.

(d) Political Murder and Revenge

This is the most obvious and elementary view taken of the play's theme. From a superficial point of view the play treats just the theme of a political murder committed with the noblest of motives and the revenge of that murder. This is the view of Adrien Bonjour.

> *Julius Caesar* is the story of a political murder and a posthumous revenge.[9]

The fact that the murder is a political one is stressed again and again. No one has any personal axe to grind, particularly

Brutus. There is envy in many hearts, particularly Cassius', and this is under evidence again and again:

> ...and this man
> Is now become a god, and Cassius is
> A wretched creature, and must bend his body
> If Caesar carelessly but nod on him.
>
> . . . .
>
> Upon what meat doth this our Caesar feed.
> That he is grown so great?
>
> . . . .
>
> A man no mightier than thyself, or me,
> In personal action, yet prodigious grown,
> And fearful.[10]

Thus, there is envy in Cassius. There may be some such emotions in the others, but there is none in Brutus. The others, though they might not like Caesar, yet never mention any personal motivation in the play. It is stressed again and again that Caesar is killed to prevent dictatorship in Rome—that is, the murder is done from purely political motives, and those are highly noble ones. Personal motives have nothing to do with it.

So the first half of the play is devoted to this murder and the "posthumous revenge" mentioned by Bonjour comes later. Revenge, for that matter, is almost always posthumous. The second half of the play is devoted to the revenge action. This revenge, unlike the murder, has personal motivation. Antony loved Caesar and is going to avenge his murder. But this is not the only personal motivation. There is the far more sordid one of gain. In the very first scene with Octavius and Lepidus, Antony talks of dividing Caesar's empire among the three of them. As a matter of fact, his grief for Caesar is not much in evidence after the Forum speech. This theme of murder and revenge affects the structure of the play as well.

(e) Personal Motivation in Politics

This point of view argues that in *Julius Caesar*, Shakespeare is studying the moral aspect of history as well as that of politics, and that in this it follows the other English chronicle plays:

> *Julius Caesar* was separated by no great distance in time from the two parts of *Henry IV* and *Henry V* and is concentrated upon the interplay of personal motives and public necessity.[11]

In studying this theme and in his attitude to history, Shakespeare is indebted to the classical historian Plutarch. It is not that he slavishly followed Plutarch, but he definitely imbibed, through Lord North's translation, Plutarch's moral outlook on history. Plutarch had (a) dramatized his heroes, giving them speeches at moments of importance, (b) selected those episodes that had a high dramatic value, and (c) believed in holding up historical events and characters as moral examples to future generations. Shakespeare was undoubtedly influenced by these factors. Moreover, his own thought-patterns reflected upon the manifold aspects of history and he treated them in his English chronicle plays. In these plays, he had presented, again and again, the figure of the king with his divine rights and all that it implied. In his Roman plays, he continued studying the same theme.

This is not an isolated example of poetic meditation upon history. It stands against a solid background of Elizabethan thought. In his time, much thought was devoted to Roman political themes, especially that of Julius Caesar. There were two groups of thoughts concerning him. One of them disliked the very thought of killing the man who had obtained a position of authority and the other school thought that a tyrant should, in any case, be eliminated. Caesar's case presented a most interesting and valid example of how such a murder might be served to turn the course of history. It was the best-known example at his time and Shakespeare treated it with due expertise.

Shakespeare, like his contemporaries, believed in the validity of order in society. This order was personified and maintained by the king and civil war meant the destruction of that order. But to look at history from this point of view is to over-simplify it, for always for a dramatist, the human, the psychological factor is very clearly present in the personality of the characters. Their actions, their motives, and feelings and emotions as well as family relationships, all are of great importance to the dramatist. Thus, he is not ready to evaluate Caesar's character or give any clear indication of how Caesar's dictatorship might turn out to be:

> The result is a play in which dramatic suspense is supported by a keen and detached insight into human motives.[12]

The fact that the play is distanced in space by being removed to Rome has made this detachment all the more possible. Shakespeare can be more impersonal and thereby more universal. This has been conveyed through the portrayal of characters because it is the psychological factor that motivates the action. He portrays Caesar as a fallible human being, superstitious, arrogant, only too ready to believe himself as set apart from other humans:

(i) Danger knows full well
That Caesar is more dangerous than he
We are two lions Litter'd in one day
And I the elder and more terrible.

(ii) If I could be well mov'd, if I were as you;
If I could pray to move, prayers would move me
But I am constant as the northern star.[13]

All this goes to prove that Shakespeare wants to portray him as a human being, not merely as a political leader. The same is true of each and every character. Even Brutus, whose nobility is taken for granted, is not portrayed as entirely noble. He too has his shortcomings which come to the fore in the quarrelling scene. The triumvirs are presented as greedy opponents. Thus, throughout the play, each of the characters is presented as a human being first, then the motives for his actions can be truly estimated. As they are themselves fallible, so are their actions. Civil war is embarked upon, which means the destruction of order and in the end, self-destruction is the only course open to the conspirators. The action they undertook because they wanted to save Rome is seen to have been a mere dream to what follows.

This is the earliest of the Roman plays and according to this critic, the theme that has been treated here is carried on in *Antony and Cleopatra* and *Coriolanus*.

(f) Triple Group-Relationship

This is the view of Geoffrey Bullough, the famous scholar whose work on the sources of Shakespeare is accepted as being the most authentic. As his main interest lies in the sources on which Shakespeare depended, he has not given discussions of any length on any other topic, but his occasional remarks are no less valuable. He is of the opinion that Shakespeare was interested, in this play, primarily in human relationships:

> *Julius Caesar* is a play about a triple group relationship—with Caesar at the centre of one group, Brutus of another, Antony of the third—and of their interactions.[14]

He supports this theory by pointing out that Shakespeare does not explore the political background of the play as he might well have done had he been interested in politics. He does not, for example, describe the Pompeian wars and the devastation they had wrought. He gives no hint of the sordid snatching at power that followed the victory at Philippi. In his English history plays he embodied, quite clearly, a moral vision of history, much as Plutarch did with Roman history, but in this play the moral content is not strong. Instead he concentrates on the human and personal aspect of the characters and actions:

> Its emphasis is not on political theory but on the traits of individual men as shown in their public connections.[15]

Looked at from this point of view, the characters as well as their actions fall into three neat divisions: (i) Caesar, Calpurnia, Antony, the Soothsayer, (ii) Brutus, Cassius, the other conspirators, Portia, Lucius, and (iii) Antony, Octavius, Lepidus and a few others. These groups are not mutually exclusive ones, for Antony is in Caesar's group in the beginning and it is only after his death that he forms a separate group. There is constant interaction among these groups. Most of the conspirators, for example appear for the first time in

Act I, sc. ii as part of Caesar's retinue and in the murder scene they talk to Caesar. Not only that—Decius, who is one of the conspirators and belongs thus to Brutus's group, comes in to meet Caesar before anyone else and persuades him, like an intimate friend, to leave the house. The other conspirators also interact with Caesar in this scene.

After the murder of Caesar, of course, he is no longer there and Antony forms his own group. Here also there is interaction between him and the characters of the second group. There are very few scenes, in fact, in which they do not meet. In the murder-scene itself Antony comes and talks with the conspirators. In the Forum scene Brutus introduces Antony to the crowd and tells them to accord him a hearing. In Act V there is the maximum of interaction between these two groups. There is the parley-scene in Act V, sc. i. Then, in the fourth scene, Antony talks to Lucilius and in the last scene Antony and Octavius find the dead body of Brutus and talk to Strato and Messala, both of whom belong to Brutus's group.

This is merely an account of how many times the different groups interact. A study of the subjects they talk about, the manner in which they talk, the influences they have on each other, the actions that are the result of their talk, the manner in which their actions affect their country—all these will show how much validity Bullough's claim has. As it is, it has been pointed out by critics again and again how much importance the personalities of these historical characters had for Shakespeare and how often he had stressed these aspects.

(g) Sub-themes

The topics discussed above pertain to the central theme of the play—the one all-important theme that holds the play together. But the word "theme" is also used in another sense, according to which it means, not the central idea, but a frequently recurring idea or a motif. This is the sense in which G. Wilson Knight has used it in his discussion:

> From the crystal fluidity...of *Julius Caesar* stand out two main persistent themes: the Brutus-theme and the Cassius-theme.[16]

He then proceeds to trace how these two characters interact with and influence each other and the other characters in the play. But this is not a study of the central theme of the play, or even of sub-themes. He has made use of the term "theme" in a sense different from that which is the objective of this chapter.

It can be seen, as in the case of genre that though the play, on the face of it, seems quite straightforward, yet critics have found a lot of complexity in it. Sometimes critics have chosen to interpret the theme in terms of other branches of art and knowledge. Hardin Craig, for example, uses terms from music:

> Shakespeare combines in a wide canvas two of these themes. In the first Caesar is cadent and Brutus crescent; in the second Brutus is cadent and Antony crescent.[17]

Here also the term "theme" has been used, not to designate the main idea in the play, but in a different sense. In fact the manner in which Hardin Craig has used it is more applicable to the plot than to the theme of the play. Derek Traversi, who has found the theme to be "the study of personal motivation in politics" (*vide* section (e) above) also finds the theme to be related to structure:

> ...which lends variety to its taut dramatic structure lies in a contrast between what men propose and what, as political beings, they in fact achieve.[18]

This is slightly different from the topic he had proposed as the central theme (discussed above). As a sub-theme, however, it is eminently acceptable, and can be quite justifiably treated as an offshoot of the main theme. It can be said that the main theme is concerned with the motivation and action of the characters whereas this sub-theme is concerned with the result of those actions. The first is the more psychological of the two, and the two are integrally related, which, indeed, they ought to be.

These three critics, G. Wilson Knight, Hardin Craig and Derek Traversi, take the term 'theme' in a limited sense so that their interpretation becomes that of a sub-theme and not of the central theme. Exactly the opposite is done by L.C. Knights. His view of the theme is so wide in scope that it takes in other plays also, which are not historical or political plays, but completely different in nature. This feature has been pointed out by L.C. Knights himself. *Julius Caesar* has this in common with:

> ...those other plays of Shakespeare—they include such different plays as *Troilus and Cressida* and *Othello*.[19]

This highly inclusive theme is basically a character study. L.C. Knights ignores the political as well as the historical nature of the play and concentrates his attention on the study of character which is, basically, the very foundation of all plays:

> ...the dramatist is posing the question of how men come to deliver themselves to illusions, of how they construct for themselves a world in which, because it is not the world of reality but a projection of their own, they inevitably come to disaster.[20]

This view neglects the political and the historical nature of the play altogether, and there are very few critics who will agree to do that. The theme proposed here can be applied to not only all plays, but other literary works like novels as well. It is a highly generalized theme and has nothing to do with *Julius Caesar* in particular.

Referring especially to the last Act, L.C. Knights points out another feature of the play which can be called a sub-theme. He calls attention to several actions and events which are basically the results of mistakes and says that these confusing actions and events depict the confusion reigning in the minds of the characters themselves:

> Shakespeare in his greater plays, makes the outward action into a mirror or symbol of events and qualities in the mind or soul.[21]

In this connection, he refers specifically to the way that Cassius's death comes about. He had asked Pindarus to tell him what is happening in his tents. Pindarus tells him that Titinius (whom Cassius himself has just now sent out to reconnoitre) is taken prisoner. On hearing this Cassius infers that they have lost the battle and commits suicide. The report, however, is a wrong one as becomes clear when Titinius comes back to him. So Cassius's death is the result of a mistake. As Titimius says:

> Alas, thou hast misconstrued every thing.[22]

L.C. Knights points out that the play is full of such mistakes and errors of judgement, the most important and fatal of them being the plot against Caesar's life:

> We may add further that the play also enforces the close connexion between error and a supposed perception of "things that are not".[23]

This sub-theme too, like the others, is related to the main historical theme and can be treated as one of the offshoots of the central theme, perhaps the most important.

Brents Stirling has studied the rituals in the play and comes to the conclusion that these rituals play such an important part in it that they can be treated as making up a sub-theme. He, of course, calls it "theme" and not sub-theme:

> The theme of incantation and ritual is thus prominent throughout *Julius Caesar*.[24]

He finds the element of ritual throughout the play, from the first scene to the last. Thus he points to the scolding given by Marullus in Act I, sc. i to the artisans for their idolatry of Caesar. At the end of the scene the two of them, he and Flavius, make a ritual of stripping the statues of Caesar of the ornaments (Like wreaths, etc.) that had been put on them. In the second scene there is the reference to the ritual race in which Antony takes part and Caesar asking him to touch Calpurnia to cure her barenness with the holy thong he carries. There are many such instances of ritualistic events he finds in the play. The most important of them, of course, is the ritual of blood-bath after Caesar's murder. The murder itself is done in a ritualistic manner, with each of them striking a blow, which has been described by Plutarch. After that, the blood-bath:

> Stoop, Romans, stoop,
> And let us bathe our hands in Caesar's blood
> Up to the elbows, and besmear our swords.[25]

The ritualistic nature of this act, which will be very effective on the stage, is highlighted by Cassius in his remark on future generations:

> Stoop then and wash. How many ages hence
> Shall this our lofty scene be acted over
> In states unborn, and accents yet unknown![26]

Then Mark Antony comes in and shakes the bloodied hands of each conspirator. Both the parts of the ritual have been highlighted by Shakespeare. Antony addresses each of them individually by name and shakes hand with him:

> Let each man render me his bloody hand.
> First, Marcus Brutus, will I shake with you
> Next, Caius Cassius, do I take your hand.[27]

Thus he shakes hand with seven of them. It too, like the blood-bath is a highly stageworthy scene. Stirling remarks:

> The murder-scene is thus hallowed by Antony in a manner which quite refutes its sanctification by the conspirators.[28]

These two are the highest points of ritual in the play, but there are many other points given by this critic. Antony's Forum speech is an example, especially the place where he points out the wounds that had killed Caesar:

> Look, in this place ran Cassius' dagger through:
> See what a rent the envious Casca made:
> Through this the well-beloved Brutus stabb'd.[29]

Referring to this passage, Stirling makes the ritualistic aspect clear:

> Holding Caesar's bloody mantle as a talisman, he reproduces seriatim the sacrificial strokes.[30]

Just as the central theme holds the play together, serving as the focus of unity, so do the sub-themes enrich the play. Most of the time the sub-themes are integrally related to the play, and sometimes are the offshoots of the main theme. Indeed, if they are completely independent of the main theme, it will add to the variety, but also give an impression of confusion. This is never the case with Shakespeare. In his plays the various themes and sub-themes are strongly welded together to create a unified whole.

NOTES

1. Paul, Stapfer, "Shakespeare and Classical Antiquity", in Ure, *op. cit.*, p. 35.
2. L.C. Knights, in Ure, *op. cit.*, p. 123.
3. *Ibid.*, p. 125.
4. Act I, sc. iii, ll. 140-41, 153-56, pp. 31-32.
5. Virgil K., Whitaker, *op. cit.*, p. 175.
6. Act II, sc. i, ll. 10-12, pp. 33-34.
7. Act III, sc. ii, ll. 22-23, 27, p. 79.
8. Act III, sc. i, ll. 104-05, p. 69; Act III, sc. i, ll. 171-72, p. 72; Act III, sc. ii, ll. 37-38, p. 79; Act IV, sc. iii, ll. 18-20, p. 98.
9. Ure, *op. cit.*, p. 19.
10. Act I, sc. ii, ll. 114-17, p. 14; Act I, sc. ii, ll. 147-48, p. 16; Act I, sc. iii, ll. 76-8, p. 28.
11. Traversi, *op. cit.*, p. 9.
12. *Ibid.*, p. 12.
13. Act II, sc. ii, ll. 44-8, pp. 53-4; Act III, sc. i, ll. 58-60, p. 54.
14. Bullough, *op. cit.*, p. 56.
15. *Ibid.*, p. 57.
16. G. Wilson Knight, *The Wheel of Fire*, London, Methuen and Co. Ltd., 1977 rpt., p. 120.
17. Hardin Craig, *The Literature of the English Renaissance*, New York, Collier Books, 1962, p. 100.
18. Derek Traversi, *op. cit.*, p. 22.
19. L.C. Knights, *Personality and Politics in Julius Caesar*, in Ure, *op. cit.*, p. 123.
20. *Ibid.*
21. *Ibid.*, p. 136.
22. Act V, sc. iii, l. 84, p. 122.
23. Knights, *op. cit.*, p. 137.
24. Brents Stirling, "Ritual in Julius Caesar" in Ure, *op. cit.*, p. 162.
25. Act III, sc. i, ll. 105-07, p. 69.
26. Act III, sc. i, ll. 111-13, p. 69
27. Act III, sc. i, ll. 184-86, p. 72.
28. Stirling, *op. cit.*, p. 166.
29. Act III, sc. ii, ll. 176-78, p. 84.
30. Stirling, *op. cit.*, p. 168.

6

The Major Characters

More than in any other field, it is in the field of characterization that Shakespeare stands unrivalled. Critics and readers have been enthralled by the different aspects of his plays, but the one of characterization has been the most productive of critical analysis. His characters are not merely lifelike and realistic—they are far more in that they are universal, often symbolic in dimensions. This is a quality rare indeed.

The other dramatists of his time also sketched great and memorable characters, but many of them spent their energy in creating the major characters, neglecting the minor ones. Shakespeare is an exception in that he pays attention to his minor characters also. No one is neglected. This creates the impression of a well-populated background against which the major characters play their roles.

It is the ambition of every dramatist and novelist to create such characters, even one or two, who can be counted among the portraits in the gallery of memorable characters in English literature. Shakespeare has added more such portraits than anyone else. There are the great tragic heroes, Hamlet, King Lear and others, heroines like Rosalind, Viola and others on one hand, and on the other the equally important villains like Iago, Shylock *et al.*

What is, perhaps, the most important point about Shakespeare's creativeness is that he never stood still, but went on developing till the last. His art went on reaching different levels of maturity and so did his character-portrayal. Thus, comparing Shakespeare's characters with Ben Jonson's Dryden says:

> The faultless Jonson equally writ well,
> Shakespeare made faults, but then did more excel.
>
> . . . .
>
> In Imitation, Jonson's wit was shown,
> Heaven made his men, but Shakespeare
> made his own.[1]

His art of character-portrayal, like his other arts, developed gradually and the early works are immature. The two pairs of lovers, for example, in *A Midsummer Night's Dream* are not as different from each other as might be desired and the witty courtiers of *Love's Labour's Lost* hardly differ from each other. It is not a noble character who stands out in these early plays but a humble one, Bottom of the *Dream*.

Characters become more and more sharply individualized as the days of experimentation are left behind. There are the important figures of the Chronicle plays with Falstaff gaining the status of uniqueness, and the female figures of the Golden Comedies. The latter gain so much importance as to overshadow their male counterparts. Paradoxically enough the only male figure to tower over everyone else in these plays is not the romantic hero, but a villain—Shylock.

The great male figures arrive with the third stage of his career. The more than lifesize figures of the tragic heroes are to be found in the great tragedies and the problem plays, in all of which he dealt with the problem of the existence and flourishing of evil in life. It is perhaps with characters like Hamlet, Macbeth, Lady Macbeth and others in mind that Pope said:

> His characters are so much Nature herself that 'tis a sort of injury to call them by so distant a name as copies of her.[2]

In the Last Romances, again, we find that his characters have undergone a change. His concern is no longer the existence of evil but man's reaction to it. Sin is inevitable, but it leads to repentance and from that to purification. The dramatist shows his heroes in throes of spiritual development following this path, emerging chastened with sorrows and sufferings. A purer, younger generation succeeds to continue the business of life. Such persons automatically gain a symbolic significance, thus ascending to a level above universality.

Such are the qualities that distinguish his characters from those of the other playwrights. One factor has to be remembered, however—the characters are not entirely his own invention. The majority of them had already existed in the sources he used. But they had mostly been vague and shadowy nonentities (except, of course, historical figures like the ones in the play under discussion). Shakespeare took them up and re-created them, endowing each of them with new life and individuality.

What is more, while depicting the characters he had to do so according to the classical rules as well as contemporary dramatic and stage conventions. Here also, he not only accepted the rules but made use of them to enhance his own works:

> It is equally undeniable that, allowing for his own peculiar genius, he conforms with the accepted conventions of character-drawing as with other conventions.[3]

The guidelines he followed were the same as were available to everyone else, yet no one created characters like his. There were the classical rules as laid down by Aristotle and Horace and expounded by the critics of Renaissance Italy. He had read classical plays in school and could find practical examples there, turning to Seneca for tragedies and Plautus and Terence for comedies. Elizabethan England itself produced several theoretical works that defined and gave examples of different kinds of characters. To name a few: Newton's *The Touchstone of Complexions*, Bishop Hall's *Characters of Virtues and Vices*, Sir Thomas Overbury's *Characters*, gave the theoretical as well as the practical aspects. These were available to everyone, but Shakespeare was the only one to create miracles that outlive the barriers of language, space and time.

To take up the classical rules, the tradition of writing character-sketches goes back to Aristotle. He had given elaborate descriptions of different types of characters in his *Nicomachaean Ethics*. Later theorists went on adding to Aristotle's list till, by the time of the Renaissance Theophrastus gave more than a hundred. Quintilian had called these sketches "set definitions of fixed characters". These present practical descriptions, and in his *Poetics* Aristotle had given rules for all characters. There are four of them: (a) Proportion, (b) Appropriateness, (c) Realism, and (d) Consistency.

The attribute of proportion is also sometimes translated as Goodness and this is because the term has a deeply moral implication. Aristotle tells that the motivation of a character must be good:

> Any speech or action that manifests moral purpose of any kind will be expressive of character: the character will be good if the purpose is good.[4]

Goodness, however, depends on the social level of the characters. Aristotle gives the following example: if a servant does not steal then he is good, but the same cannot be said about a gentleman whose social level and standard are different. Shakespeare excels in portraying this trait. In the play under discussion all the characters are historical ones, yet even here he has observed this Aristotelian rule. Bullough points out:

> What Shakespeare learned from Plutarch was to represent more clearly than before the paradoxes of human motives, the mixture of good and evil in the same person.[5]

Appropriateness or Propriety is the second trait. A character should act or speak according to his nature. Again Aristotle gives an example:

> There is a type of manly valour; but valour in a woman or unscrupulous cleverness is inappropriate.[6]

Shakespeare observes this rule, for his characters never act or speak "out of characters". Brutus is uniformly noble. Caesar is portrayed as arrogant, and he is always so. Antony is loyal, but greedy for power.

Aristotle has not paid much attention to the third quality, Realism. He points out that it is different from goodness and propriety but he does not explain it further except to say that a character should be true to life. Herein Shakespeare's expertise is unrivalled. M.C. Bradbrook has laid stress upon it:

> Shakespeare's innovations in character-drawing may be compared to the introduction of perspective in painting: he gave the illusion of life.[7]

The fourth attribute given is that of Consistency. This is the most important one of all four and means that a character must be true to his self and remain so without any drastic changes. It is true that there are some cases of a drastic change of heart in Shakespeare. He did not always follow the rules, but changed them according to the demands of the play. What Pope said in this connection should be kept in mind:

> To judge therefore of Shakespeare by Aristotle's rules is like trying a man by the laws of one country, who acted under those of another.[8]

Apart from these, some other rules have been given for the towering figure of the tragic hero. In addition to these rules, Shakespeare had the examples of Latin and English tragic heroes before him: those of Seneca, Kyd and Marlowe, let alone other, lesser known writers. The rules given by Aristotle for the tragic hero, in addition to the four already mentioned are: the tragic hero must be better than the average, of noble birth and nature and he must have some kind of flaw in his nature. This last is the most important trait of all. The Elizabethans understood it as the tragic flaw which brings doom and destruction upon the hero. Aristotle specifically points out that it is not a serious moral flaw:

> A man who is not eminently good and just, yet whose misfortune is brought about not by vice or depravity but by some error or frailty.[9]

"Hamartia", which is the actual term made famous by Aristotle, means an error of judgement that brings about the fall of the hero. This error of judgement, in later drama, came to mean a serious flaw in the character like procrastination in Hamlet, jealousy in Othello, etc. It need not, however, encompass such destructive traits. Any serious moral flaw detracts from the dignity of the hero, but a mere error of judgement does not imperil his nobility. Aristotle is careful to preserve the nobility and insists that the hero must be better than the average man:

> Tragedy is an imitation of persons who are above the common level.... The poet, in representing men who are irascible or indolent, or have such other defects of character, should present the type and yet ennoble it.[10]

The character of Brutus is truly that of an ideal tragic hero from the Aristotelian point of view.

When we start considering the characters of Julius Caesar, one thing should be kept in mind: these are all historical figures, as is the case with the English chronicle plays also. In both of these cases Shakespeare had to follow the accounts given by historians, Plutarch in the case of this play. This was a tricky problem, for he had to keep to the historically known facts and create a living character out of them. This feature has been put very succinctly by J.I.M. Stewart. He says that there are two levels to the play or two "planes":

> ...The planes upon which Shakespeare builds: the simple outward and heroic plane upon which men show themselves to the world like figures on a stage; the complex and inward plane along which we are drawn to a knowledge of the hidden man.[11]

In this respect, moreover, Horace has something extremely pertinent to say. He refers to the mythical character Achilles, but what he says applies to the present case as well:

> Either follow the beaten track, or invent something that is consistent within itself. If in your play you happen to be representing the illustrious Achilles, let him be energetic, passionate, ruthless and implacable.[12]

He has taken the example of Achilles to clarify what is to be done if the dramatist is depicting a well-known figure. As such, the main principle given here will apply to the characters in our play. It can be said that here the dramatist adopts both of the two ways pointed out by Horace, he "follows the beaten track" in being faithful to the picture presented by Plutarch and also "invents something that is consistent within itself". He does it with so much insight and art that the characters emerge as both historically true and realistically acceptable.

The characters of *Julius Caesar* are now to be considered individually. Usually, in a tragedy, it is the hero's character which is the first to be considered. In this play, it is doubtful who the hero is. Most of the critics say it is Brutus though Caesar is the titular hero. As has been pointed out by several scholars, it is not necessary for a historical play to be centred around one single hero:

> In a historical play, as conceived by Shakespeare, the single hero... is not essential.... There is in *Julius Caesar*, no bright particular star dimming the glory of all his fellows in the firmament.[13]

This is perfectly true. The difficulty arises in the case of *Julius Caesar* because it is not an ordinary history play but a tragedy, and tragedies are always hero-centred plays.

(a) Julius Caesar

Julius Caesar is the titular hero of the play, though it is very doubtful whether he is the dramatic hero as well—as, for example, Hamlet, or Macbeth, or Othello are. That honour goes to Brutus.

The main reason for this ambivalence is that Caesar departs this world and the play half way through it. Thereafter he appears as a Ghost and exercises great posthumous effect upon the action, yet it is difficult to give him the status of the hero. A few of the critical opinions on him will make this clear:

> (i) We do not much admire the representation here given of Julius Caesar.... He makes, several vapouring and rather pedantic speeches and does nothing.
>
> (ii) Caesar himself is, in Shakespeare, almost a failure.

(iii) If Shakespeare were a modern writer, I should be more clear about his conceptions, I should be certain that he is planning Caesar to be little in life and great in death.

(iv) Caesar is revealed in fact, less as brave and consistent, than as talking himself into consistency.

(v) Caesar's triumphs are in the past, and his aura of greatness seems insubstantial.

(vi) A Roman Tamburlaine of illimitable ambition and ruthlessly irresistible general.[14]

The majority of the critics are inclined to take this rather derogatory view of him. This view is not a very mistaken one, for Shakespeare takes pains to present him as a fallible human being. One reason is the attitude in the source:

> From the first eight hundred words of the *Life of Caesar*, Shakespeare had learnt three things, each conveyed through the medium of narration: Caesar was fearless; he was possessed of a histrionic streak and fond of making speeches; he was ruthless. And what later emerges is equally simple. Caesar had a covetous desire to be called king, and was resisted by Brutus.[15]

Shakespeare not only highlights each of these traits, but, in consistency with them, following Horace, puts in some speeches and actions, so that, as a whole, Caesar emerges as a fully rounded-out individual. This is the more to be admired as he has modified Plutarch in many particulars in his presentation. There are many unfavourable incidents given by Plutarch which he does not even mention. In fact his portrayal of Caesar is far kinder than the one given by Plutarch. The classical historian, for example, admits that the soldiers of his army admired his courage but puts a derogatory remark in:

> Further more, they did not wonder so much at his valliantnesse in putting himself at every instant in such manifest daunger...knowing that it was his greedie desire of honour that set him a fire.[16]

Moreover, Shakespeare presents the matter of conspiracy as being organized only by a few of the aristocrats, and that too as a matter of principle, not out of hatred. There is envy in Casca, but he is the only one presented in this manner. Plutarch, on the other hand, clearly marks it out that Caesar was generally hated on Rome:

> But the chiefest cause that made him mortally hated, was the covetous desire he had to be called king, which first gave the people just cause and next his secret enemies honest colour to bear him ill-will.[17]

This sentence by Plutarch implies several things: (a) that Caesar inspired strong hatred, (b) it was because he wanted to be the king, (c) that the "general people" had "just cause", and (d) he had secret enemies. All these are toned down by Shakespeare. In fact, he gives the second and the fourth factors, leaving out the first and the third.

We see him first in Act I, sc. ii. He shows himself as a man who has faith in religious rites since he asks Antony to touch Calpurnia while running in the feast of the Lupercalia and then the Soothsayer comes. Caesar does not take him seriously at all. This first meeting is not given in Plutarch's account.

After this, he goes out and then place the incident of Antony offering him a crown. This happens offstage and he enters again. It is here that he declares his preference for fat men and also expresses his great self-regard. He thinks himself to be greater than Cassius and declares "for always I am Caesar".

We see him next after two scenes. Here, he is shown at first in a domestic scene—not as a dictator but as a husband. He listens to Calpurnia's dreams and at first they do not move him. When he hears that the animal which has been sacrificed at the temple did not have a heart, even then he is unshakeable in his not having a heart, even then he is unshakeable in his determination to go to the Senate. As a matter of fact, he says that no less than five times in this scene, up till this speech. Then abruptly, his attitude changes once more. Pleadings by Calpurnia succeed and he decides not to go out. Then, when Decius comes and gives him a favourable interpretation of Calpurnia's dream and holds out the inducement of a crown, he changes his mind again. This proves that he is motivated by greed for the crown which is so strong as to overcome all fears.

It becomes noticeable in this scene that he talks of himself in the third person. He does so ten times in this scene. His whole attitude in this scene is eloquent of the enormous value he puts on himself. He has already assumed the airs of a dictator:

> Decius, go tell them Caesar will not come.
>
> ... ...
>
> The cause is in my will, I will not come;
> That is enough to satisfy the senate.[18]

His behaviour in this scene is already that of a king. This becomes even more heightened when we see him next, in the murder scene (Act III, sc. i). Here he first of all challenges the senate, then refuses to go through the suits presented to him and withdraws into the senate. Now when Metellus pleads for his brother Caesar's *hybris* shows itself at its worst. Again and again he shows that he regards himself as superior to others. He says that in fixity of purpose he is like the pole star. About this H.S. Wilson remarks that it:

> seems in itself enough to provoke the thrusts of the conspirators.[19]

He spurns Brutus and likens himself to the Olympus. It is then that the conspirators stab him. Plutarch describes how, at first, he tried to save himself. Then, seeing that Brutus too has stabbed him he gave up his famous last words, "Et tu, Brute", however, have not been given by Plutarch. It is Suetonius who gives his last words, and, though addressed to Brutus, they are in Greek, not Latin as given by Shakespeare, meaning: "And thou, my son"?

Shakespeare, thus, has not glorified him, but presented him as a fallible human being like anybody else. But he fancied himself to be far greater:

> In Shakespeare's rendering of the character of Caesar... one thought of the poet had seemed to be this—that unless a man continually keeps himself in relation with

> facts he may become to himself legendary and mythical.[20]

(b) Brutus

Though Caesar is the titular hero of the play, Brutus is generally regarded as the real or the dramatic hero. This general view is expressed by K. Muir:

> Caesar is the victim, not the hero. The hero is, of course, Brutus, "the noblest Roman of them all.[21]

He has, in fact, all the qualities of the Aristotelian hero: he is physically present in twelve of the eighteen scenes of the play. His nobility is a by-word in the play. There is great conflict in him, and his end generates both pity and terror in the reader and the audience. His *hamartia* is *hamartia* in the true Aristotelian sense in that it was an error of judgement that led him to make the choice of joining the conspirators which turned out to be so tragically wrong. All in all, he can be called the ideal tragic hero in the Aristotelian sense:

> The Elizabethan tragedy of Brutus, like that of Othello, is marked by an integrity of conduct which leads the protagonist into evil and measures him in his error.[22]

This expresses, roughly, the opinion of the majority of Shakespearean critics. There are, however, a few voices of denigration as well:

> (a) Brutus is nothing but a familiar type of English suburban preacher: politically he would hardly impress the Thames Conservancy Board.
>
> ... ...
>
> (b) But Brutus is not the centre and soul of the play.... In the first scene Brutus is not so much as mentioned.[23]

It is perfectly true that in the other tragedies the hero, even if he is not present on the stage in the first scene, is all the same present in the dialogue of the other characters in such a way that there is no doubt in anyone's mind about his prominence in the play. But Brutus is not even mentioned in the opening scene.

We thus see him first, not in the opening scene, but in the second scene of Act I. The beginning of this scene, too, like the entire preceding scene, is devoted to Caesar. Then with 25 lines, the second part of the scene, the focus shifts and Brutus and Cassius come to the centre of the stage. In the dialogue that ensues we see Cassius taking the active part while Brutus remains passive. Cassius is trying to persuade Brutus to join the conspirators, but not openly. In fact he does not mention the conspiracy, but tries first to sound Brutus as to his attitude and later appeals to his nobility and patriotism. Brutus shows himself responsive to his overtures and after listening to Casca later in the scene he goes away but not before promising to meet Cassius. As Cassius remarks immediately afterwards, Brutus shows himself pliable to the suggestions thrown out by him and when we see him next he has already decided, not only to join the conspiracy but also to kill Caesar:

> It must be by his death: and for my part,
> I know no personal cause to spurn at him,
> But for the general.[24]

This soliloquy has been interpreted in many ways by many critics. Coleridge was puzzled by it, for it seemed to express ignoble ideas:

> Surely nothing can seem more discordant with our historical pre-conception of Brutus, or more lowering to the intellect of this Stoico-Platonic tyrannicide, than the tenets here attributed to him.[25]

After this, there have been many different explanations of this soliloquy. What actually happens, however, is that, after cogitating for some time and justifying his choice to himself he goes back to the views with which he had opened the scene—to kill Caesar.

Lucius then brings one of the anonymous messages strew in his house. Cassius had decided to do this, and it is given in Plutarch as well. This one appeals to his pride in his ancient lineage and helps confirm his resolutions. It is this resolution that represents his error of judgement, his *hamartia*. As Stapfer had said in the nineteenth century.

> Had the empire depended only upon the generalship of one man, Brutus, in killing Caesar, might have saved the Republic, but in point of fact the Empire was rooted in the general state of things. It was in not perceiving this that the error of Brutus lay, and from this also resulted the utter failure of his enterprise.[26]

Other critics have found different reasons, but all agree that it was the wrong choice to make. The play has been interpreted as a morality play and from that point of view, this is a crucial choice that spells either salvation or damnation, and Brutus makes the wrong choice (*vide* Chap. 4, *supra*, the section on Genre).

After this, the conspirators enter and they confer together. Cassius proposes a swearing ceremony but Brutus opposes it and proceeds to glorify the intended murder by elevating it to patriotism. This is expressive of his nobility if a positive view is taken, whereas, according to the negative view, it is merely self-deception. Indeed his character has been interpreted as of one who is continually and foolishly deceiving himself.

The same nobility that tends to avoid anything sordid and ignoble makes him spare Antony. Here again, he appeals to the inherent nobility of his fellow-conspirators by saying that killing Antony will make their action "seem too bloody" and they must make it clear to the Romans that they have killed Caesar, and Caesar only, in order to save the Republic.

This again is a wrong choice. As a matter of fact, Brutus goes on making wrong choices, taking the wrong decision, again and again. He will do the same in the murder-scene, by granting Antony permission to speak. Every time the choice leads to disaster. Plutarch has especially pointed out these mistakes:

> For the first fault he did was, when he would not consent to his fellow conspirators, that Antonius should be stained.... The second fault was, when he agreed that Caesar's funerals should be as Antonius would have then: the which in deede marred all.[27]

When the conspirators leave, an entirely different aspect of Brutus reveals itself. He finds the servant Lucius asleep and instead of rousing or rebuking him speaks tenderly to him. Then Portia comes in and we see Brutus as a tender and considerate husband. He had been very perturbed and restless the past few days but had not said anything to her for he did not want her to worry over him. Even now, he wants to spare her anxiety and tells her that he is not quite well and that is why he has been behaving rather oddly. Portia importunes him to confide in her but before he can do so Igarius comes in and both of them go out.

Comparing Brutus with Cassius as both of them appear in the two domestic scenes, Musgrove finds the former far superior to the latter:

> Caesar compares most unfavourably with Brutus when he meets him on his own ground.... He neither treats her as an equal, as Brutus had treated Portia, nor does he comfort her as her fearful nature requires.[28]

He is seen in the next scene only to speak a few words (two and half lines) and then in the murder-scene. After the killing of Caesar, it is he who keeps his cool and reassures the other senators, and after a few lines suggests the blood-bath:

> Stoop, Romans, stoop,
> And let us bathe our hands in Caesar's blood
> Up to the elbows, and besmear our swords:
> Then walk we forth, even to the market-place,
> And waving our red weapons O'er our heads,
> Let's all cry, "Peace, freedom, and liberty"![29]

He has not only converted the murder into a holy ritual, but also proclaimed the unselfish and noble motives behind it. This ritual of the blood-bath has been interpreted in many ways, some of them detrimental to Brutus, as expressing his self-deception:

> Brutus was a man who thought that an abstract "common good" could be achieved without due regard to the complexity of the actual.[30]

After this comes the confrontation with Antony. Brutus, throughout the meeting behaves with the nobility natural to him, justifying their deed as having been done from democratic and patriotic motives:

> Our hearts you see not; they are pitiful;
> And pity to the general wrong of Rome—
> As fire drives out fire, so pity pity—
> Hath done this deed on Caesar.[31]

Then he makes his second serious, almost fatal mistake: he allows Antony to speak at Caesar's funeral. It is true that he imposes conditions which seem at the time to be foolproof, but, as Shakespeare shows, they are easily got over.

His own speech is a model of classical prose. Each sentence is meticulously divided and balanced. The appeal is to the intellect. It has been pointed out that there is a subtle kind of flattery in his speech—that he pays his audience, the compliment of considering them to be on the same level as himself, and they respond favourably:

> The very fact that he does not talk down to them, will not speak their language as Antony does is a compliment to their intelligence.[32]

But Antony is a demagogue and soon has the mob in a frenzy against the conspirators. As E.M. Forster says:

> Brutus is an intellectual who can do things... he can do things, but he always does them wrong.[33]

Then we have the quarrelling-scene. Dryden has compared it with like scenes from Euripides and Fletcher, showing two noblemen quarrelling and then being reconciled. Wilson Knight is of the opinion that it is "exquisitely human and pathetic".

It is true that Cassius provokes the quarrel, but Brutus does not shine in it either. He accuses Cassius of having an "itching palm" and torments him:

> Must I observe you? Must I stand and crouch
> Under your testy humour? By the gods,
> You shall digest the venom of your spleen.
> Though it do split you.[34]

Pointing to these lines, Derek Traversi remarks that these reveal unpleasant sides of Brutus's character. His argument is that there has always been a trace of egoism in Brutus, and this is what comes to the surface here:

> There is pleasure in inflicting humiliation...moral callousness born of self-sufficiency...and contempt.... The element of egoism present from the first beneath Brutus's noble façade is coming to the surface.[35]

Then of course, both of them realize that this quarrel will only spell disaster and then they make it up. The interruption afforded by the Poet helps in the reconciliation.

It is after this that, Brutus tells Cassius about Portia's death. He shows true stoic control over himself: "speak no more of her". His love for Portia is genuine, but he represses all outward show of it:

> If the philosopher in him dictates this assumption of emotional control, the husbands' affection warns him not to give voice to a feeling which, once expressed, might shatter all containing limits.[36]

What is puzzling is that this revelation takes place again when Titinius and Messala come in. Brutus pretends as if he did not know about Portia's death and asks Messala about it. It has been suggested that he does this because he is hoping against hope that the earlier news he had had may be false.

It is decided that they will meet at Philippi from whence the battle will start. Then, when Brutus is ready for rest, the Ghost comes. Brutus takes it for a hallucination at first. Then he talks to it and is told that it is his evil spirit and that they will meet again at Philippi. By this time he believes that it is not imagination, that he is really seeing Caesar's Ghost. It vanishes very quickly and Brutus asks his servants if they had seen anything. They had not. It is true that the Ghost does not say that he will be defeated in the battle, but its very appearance makes Brutus have premonitions of disaster.

After this, there is the parley-scene which fails, and battle follows. Brutus and Cassius bid farewell to each other and they do not meet again. Cassius kills himself and Brutus does the same. It is left for Antony to deliver the epitaph on him:

> This was the noblest Roman of them all.
>
> . . . .
>
> His life was gentle, and the elements
> So mix'd in him, that Nature might stand up
> And say to all the world, "This was a man".[37]

This encomium is not bestowed on him by Shakespeare alone but, as Plutarch says, not only Antony but everyone honoured Brutus, even his enemies:

> But for Brutus, his verie enemies themselves confessed, that of all those that conspired Caesar's death, he only had no other ende and intent to attempt his enterprise, but to restore the empire of Rome again to her former self and government.[38]

(c) Caius Cassius

Cassius is the most important of the conspirators and, as Hazlitt had observed, in comparison with Brutus:

> Cassius is better cut out for a conspirator, his heart prompted his head. His habit made him fear the worst that might happen and his irritability of temper added to his inveteracy of purpose and sharpened his patriotism.[39]

On the other hand, Shaw, who denigrates everyone, and everything in the play, say: "Cassius is a vehemently assertive nonentity".[40] Everyone, however, agrees that Shakespeare himself has given the best analysis of his character through Caesar. Coming back from the festival Caesar says:

> Yond Cassius has a lean and hungry look;
> He thinks too much: such men are dangerous.
> . . . . . . He reads much
> He is a great observer, and he looks
> Quite through the deeds of other men
>
> . . . .
>
> Such men are never at heart's ease
> Whiles they behold a greater than themselves.[41]

As in the case of the other characters, Shakespeare has based his portrayal of Cassius also on Plutarch. There are several indications in Plutarch's *Life of Brutus* on the kind of personality Cassius had:

> Cassius being a chollericke man, and hating Caesar privatelie, more then he did the tyrannie openlie: he incensed Brutus against him.
>
> . . . .
>
> Cassius even from his cradell could not abide any man of tyrans, as it appeared when he was but a boy.[42]

These three traits of Cassius's character: choleric temper, hatred of Caesar, and hatred of tyranny have all been faithfully given by Shakespeare, as a brief study of his speeches and actions will show.

We see him first in Act I sc. ii when he enters in Caesar's train along with most of the characters in the play. It is when he is left alone with Brutus, that his character starts to unfold. The conspirators have already got together and they want Brutus with them. Now Cassius is trying to know Brutus's mind. He starts by praising him and when Brutus uses the word "fear" in connection with Caesar's being chosen the king, he at once pounces upon it:

> Ay, do you fear it?
> Then must I think you would not have it so.[43]

After this he tells two anecdotes about Caesar, proving that he is not a demi-god or anything like that, but a weak mortal like other men:

> I was born free as Caesar, so were you;
> We both have fed as well, and we can both
> Endure the winter's cold as well as he.[44]

He stresses the weakness and fallibility of Caesar again and again, and this speaks eloquently of the second trait mentioned by Plutarch: hatred of Caesar. Shakespeare brings to the fore the envy that Cassius feels that Caesar, being like them, has yet grown to such a stature that everyone is in awe of him:

And this man
Is now become a god, and Cassius is
A wretched creature and must bend his body

. . . .

Why, man, he doth bestride the narrow world
Like a Colossus, and we petty men
Walk under his huge legs.

. . . .

Upon what meat doth this our Caesar feed,
That he is grown so great?[45]

This is fully in keeping with the traits given by Plutarch. But, to be just, Cassius blames, not only Caesar, but also themselves, in the famous lines:

The fault, Dear Brutus, is not in our stars,
But in ourselves, that we are underlings.[46]

He reflects on the fact that the age itself has got degenerated, that the Romans themselves have got corrupted. It is the typical attitude of a satirist, what Traversi calls a "combination of idealism and personal resentment" that Cassius most successfully uses to win Brutus over.

Then Caesar enters with his train, gives his most appropriate sketch of Cassius and goes away. Casca tells the story of Caesar refusing the crown. Then Brutus leaves, after arranging with Cassius to meet him. In the soliloquy delivered by Cassius, he shows that he has taken Brutus's measure: that he is persuadable. He then decides to leave some anonymous notes in Brutus's house to make him decide to join the conspiracy. This has been given by Plutarch.

He takes a leading role in the next scene also, when he interprets the supernatural omens to Casca, that they all point at Caesar. Here his hatred of tyranny is manifest. Then Cinna comes and Cassius entrusts him with one of the papers he has prepared for Brutus, and leaves for the meeting of the conspirators.

The next scene shows Brutus joining the conspiracy and the sketching out of the future course of action. It is he who proposes, supported by Decius, that Antony also should be killed, but this is vetoed by Brutus.

In the murder-scene he is jittery and nervous, becoming apprehensive when Pompilius Lena indirectly makes it clear that he knows about the conspiracy. After the murder he speaks the memorable lines about future re-enactment of the murder and blood-bath:

> How many ages hence
> Shall this our lofty scene be acted over
> In states unborn and accents yet unknown.[47]

It is the consciousness of the glorious role of the stage in perpetuating human history that manifests itself here. This sentiment has been echoed by Nashe in his *Pierce Pennilesse His Supplication to the Divell* in which he imagines Talbot:

> ...after he had lyne two hundred yeare in his Tombe, he should triumphe againe on the stage and have his bones newe embalmed with the teares of ten thousand spectators.[48]

After Mark Antony has come in and has been given permission to express doubts. But this perspicacity goes in vain, for he is overridden by Brutus.

We see him next just before the quarrelling scene. He starts accusing Brutus in front of everyone and then they withdraw into the privacy of Brutus's tent where they have a violent quarrel. Then realizing the grave danger to which they are heading (for a rift between them at this juncture will spoil the whole enterprise), they get reconciled. In this quarrel, more than in anything else, Plutarch has assured us that he was a choleric man. Then, like all choleric men, he is quick to get pacified and as soon as he hears of Portia's death he is not only generous enough to forgive Brutus whole-heartedly, but even blames himself: "How scaped I killing, when I crossed you so?"[49] During the planning out of battle strategies he makes his sensible contributions but is again over-ridden by Brutus.

His next important speech comes in Act V, sc. i when he discloses to Messala that it is his birthday and tells him of the ominous portents that presage defeat for their army. There is a very fine remark by G. Wilson Knight on this:

> Cleopatra-like, he thus celebrates his birth-day under the shadow of impending death.[50]

Then the battle begins and we see him in the next scene but one. Here, he is told that Mark Antony has captured his tent and has set it afire. He sends Titinius to find out about the battle and his slave Pindarus tells him from a vantage-point that Titinius has been taken prisoner. This convinces Cassius that they are defeated. Then, with the help of Pindarus he commits suicide like a noble Roman, with the very sword that had helped kill Caesar. As it turns out the news of defeat was a wrong one, for though Cassius's army was defeated by Antony, Octavius was in turn defeated by Brutus. Both Titinius and Messala mourn the death of Cassius that is seen to be the result of a mistake. Shakespeare adapts the words which, in Plutarch, Brutus had spoken over the dead body:

> The last of all the Romans, fare thee well!
> It is impossible that ever Rome
> Should breed thy fellow. Friends, I owe more tears
> To this dead man than you shall see me pay.[51]

In Cassius, we have a character developed from just a few hints given by Plutarch. We have an able conspirator, a staunch friend, a noble Roman. Shakespeare has portrayed him like a fully rounded-out, convincing human being. It is particularly in the second half of the play that his good qualities come to the fore:

> Even in this portrait of an arch-conspirator, Shakespeare compensates weakness with strength, evil qualities with good.[52]

(d) Mark Antony/Marcus Antonius

Mark Antony has been portrayed as a devoted follower of Caesar, so devoted as to seem sycophantic. Yet after Caesar's death another facet of his personality comes to the fore: his diplomacy and thirst for power. As a matter of fact it is after

Caesar's death that he gains importance, before that he is just the faithful follower of Caesar. Shakespeare had not given any indication of the diplomacy and power-lust that was latent in him. These traits in his character, however, are not Shakespeare's invention. In one of the sources cited by Bullough, there is a play *IL Cesare* by Orlando Pescetti in which Cassius says in the conspiracy scene that Antony has a thirst for power:

> Methinks I have perceived in Antony
> Desire for power; hence, if we would secure
> Our land in every way, let us dispatch him.[53]

When Brutus does not agree and says that Antony is too pleasure-loving to be a serious threat, Cassius gives a short portrait of him:

> Antony
> Is certainly to ease and pleasure vowed,
> But on the other hand no man exists
> Stronger or more courageous.[54]

Antony's love of pleasure has been mentioned by Shakespeare in the first part of the play when Caesar compares him with Cassius ("He loves no plays,/ As thou dost, Antony"). Shakespeare also mentions his abilities in diplomacy when Cassius says in the conspiracy scene:

> We shall find of him
> A shrewd contriver; and you know his means
> If he improve them, may well stretch so far
> As to annoy us all.[55]

In the first half of the play, however, he does not shine. In fact in the few lines he speaks before Caesar's death (just thirty-three words in all) he shows a disastrous inability to judge Cassius's character:

> Fear him not, Caesar, he is not dangerous
> He is a noble Roman and well given.[56]

It is a grave mistake on his part to underestimate Cassius and Dorsch calls it an "error of judgement". Harley Granville-Barker has observed:

> Shakespeare keeps him in ambush throughout the first part of the play.[57]

As a matter of fact, Granville-Barker finds in him the portrait of the typical "good fellow", a sportsman who has turned to politics. He finds the message sent by Antony through a messenger after Caesar's death extremely significant from this point of view. Though the character has been sketched by Plutarch, yet, Granville-Barker holds that, in a way he is recognizably English:

> ...to English eyes there can be no more typically English figure than the sportsman turned statesman, but a sportsman still.[58]

His personality starts emerging after the assassination of Caesar even before he has entered the stage, for he sends his servant with a most carefully worded message calculated not to offend, yet dignified:

> Mark Antony shall not love Caesar dead
> So well as Brutus living; but will follow
> The fortunes and affairs of noble Brutus.[59]

Many critics have found this to be a crucial point in the play. Thus, at the end of the nineteenth century, in 1898, R.G. Moulton had remarked:

> In the whole Shakespeare Drama, there is nowhere such a swift swinging-round of a dramatic action as is here marked by this sudden up-springing of the suppressed individuality in Antony's character.[60]

Barely thirty years later, Granville-Barker, in 1927, repeats the same idea:

> The servant's entrance with Antony's message, checking the conspirators triumph, is the turning point of the play.[61]

When, reassured by Brutus, he does come in, his diplomacy comes to the fore. He shows grief for Caesar yet is ready to be persuaded to join the conspirators if convinced of the justice of their cause. He even offers his own life to them. Then he shakes hand with them and pretends he is won over to them when they explain their motives and then asks permission for delivering a funeral oration. It is granted with some reservations: that he shall speak after Brutus, he will not criticise the conspirators but is free to praise Caesar.

After the conspirators have gone he makes his stand clear to the audience and speaks the famous curse:

> A curse shall light upon the limbs of men;
> Domestic fury and fierce civil strife
> Shall cumber all the parts of Italy.[62]

When Octavius's servant comes, he at once sends the news of the assassination, telling him that at present, Rome is not safe for him. His grief for Caesar is genuine, but he does not allow the grief to render him inactive.

The Forum speech has been studied in detail many times. Persons other than literary critics have also acknowledged its effectiveness:

> What Shakespeare has so well caught is Antony's attempt to allay the fears of the senate and, at the same time, rouse the feelings of the mob.[63]

After this, his diplomacy and lust for power becomes clear and is expressed most unscrupulously in the scene in which he sends Lepidus out and then conspires with Octavius how to make use of him and then discard him. His diplomacy and ruthlessness, both are manifest in this scene.

He shows nobility however, when the soldiers bring Lucilius to him. He does not rebuke them and orders Lucilius to be well looked after. He shows generosity and the ability to appreciate nobility in other in his epitaph on Brutus. Granville-Barker is full of praise of Shakespeare's portrait of Antony:

> Never for a moment to let slip from our sight, the complete and complex Antony, impulsive and calculating, warm-hearted and callous that will be for the actor an achievement indeed.[64]

These are the important characters of the play. Each of them is a fully rounded-out, three-dimensional person. But his minor characters also are not neglected—each of them also, on a smaller scale, in a lesser way, is an individualized character. While following his source and the classical rules as well as contemporary conventions, Shakespeare created living human beings who are individualized as well as universalized.

NOTES

1. J. Kinsley, ed., *The Poems and Fables of John Dryden*, Oxford University Press, 1970, p. 142.
2. Quoted by Fluchere, *op. cit.*, p. 131.
3. *Ibid.*, p. 136.
4. S.H. Butcher, *Aristotle's Theory of Poetry and Fine Art with a Critical Text translation of the Poetics*, New Delhi, Kalyani Publications., 1981, p. 53.
5. Bullough, *op. cit.*, p. 57.
6. Butcher, *op. cit.*, p. 53.
7. M.C. Bradbrook, *The Growth and Structure of Elizabethan Comedy*, London, Chatto and Windus, 1955, p. 80.
8. Louis Kronenberger, ed., *Alexander Pope: Selected Works*, New York, The Modern Library, 1951, pp. 353-54.
9. Butcher, *op. cit.*, p. 45.
10. *Ibid.*, p. 57.
11. J.I.M. Stewart, *Character and Motive in Julius Caesar*, in Ure, *op. cit.*, p. 113.
12. T.S. Dorsch, transl., *Classical Literary Criticism*, Penguin Books, 1975 rpt., p. 83.
13. Mark Hunter, in Ure, *op. cit.*, p. 197.
14. (i) Hazlitt, quoted in Dorsch, *op. cit.*, p. xxvii; (ii) C.H. Herford, in Ure, *op. cit.*, p. 51; (iii) E.M. Forster, in Ure, *op. cit.*, p. 64; (iv) Traversi, *op. cit.*, p. 42; (v) Emma Smith, *op. cit.*, p. 6; (vi) Dover Wilson, quoted in Dorch, *op. cit.*, p. xxvii.
15. Traversi, *op. cit.*, p. 113.
16. Bullough, *op. cit.*, p. 66.
17. *Ibid.*, p. 80.
18. Act II, sc. ii, ll. 68-72, p. 55.
19. H.S. Wilson, *op. cit.*, p. 91.
20. Edward Dowden, in Ure, *op. cit.*, p. 33.
21. Muir, *op. cit.*, p. 46.
22. Brent Stirling, *Ritual in Julius Caesar*, in Ure, p. 160.

23. Shaw in Ure, *op. cit.*, p. 40; (b) Mark Hunter, *Brutus and the Political Context*, *ibid.*, pp. 197-98.
24. Act II, sc. i, ll 10-13, pp. 33-34.
25. Ure, *op. cit.*, p. 31.
26. *Ibid.*, p. 35.
27. Bullough, *op. cit.*, p. 104.
28. Ure, *op. cit.*, pp. 57-58.
29. Act III, sc. i, ll. 105-10, p. 69.
30. L.C. Knights, in Ure, *op. cit.*, pp. 137-38.
31. Act III, sc. i, ll. 169-72, pp. 71-72.
32. Ure, *op. cit.*, p. 184.
33. *Ibid.*, p. 63.
34. Act IV, sc. iii, ll. 45-48, p. 100.
35. Traversi, *op. cit.*, p. 63.
36. *Ibid.*, p. 67.
37. Act V, sc. v, ll. 68-75, p. 129.
38. Bullogh, *op. cit.*, p. 134.
39. Ure, *op. cit.*, p. 32.
40. *Ibid.*, p. 40
41. Act I, sc. ii, ll. 191-207, pp. 18-19.
42. Bullogh, *op. cit.*, pp. 94-95.
43. Act I, sc. ii, ll. 79-80, p. 12.
44. Act I, sc. ii, ll. 96-98, p. 13.
45. Act I, sc. ii, ll. 114-16, p. 14, ll. 133-55, p. 15, ll. 147-48, p. 16.
46. Act I, sc. ii, ll. 138-9, pp. 15-16.
47. Act III, sc. i, ll. 111-13, p. 69.
48. Ure, *op. cit.*, p. 79.
49. Act IV, sc. iii, ll. 149, p. 104.
50. Ure, *op. cit.*, p. 51.
51. Act V, sc. iii, ll. 99-102, p. 123.
52. Dorsch, *op. cit.*, p. xlvi.
53. Bullough, *op. cit.*, p. 180.
54. *Ibid.*, p. 181.

55. Act II, sc. i, ll. 157-60, p. 42.
56. Act I, sc. ii, ll. 193-94, p. 18.
57. Ure, *op. cit.*, p. 234.
58. *Ibid.*
59. Act III, sc. i, ll. 132-35, p. 70.
60. Ure, *op. cit.*, pp. 36-37.
61. *Ibid.*, p. 235.
62. Act III, sc. i, ll. 262-64, p. 76.
63. R.A.G. Carson, *History Today*, in Ure, *op. cit.*, p. 75.
64. *Ibid.*, p. 238.

7

The Minor Characters

It had been pointed out in the last chapter that, unlike many of his contemporaries, Shakespeare did not neglect his minor characters. Most of the other dramatists of his time created a few characters of overpowering importance, but the others remained more or less shadowy—Marlowe being the best example of such a writer. With Shakespeare however, this is not the case, for even his minor characters are well-rounded, convincing figures. The minor persons of the play under discussion not only provide the relevant social background, they also take the action forward. It being a historical play, there are many of them (no less than thirty-seven of them excluding the Ghost of Caesar), and Shakespeare has endowed them with the individuality appropriate to each. Only a few of them shall be discussed below, in the order in which they appear in the *Dramatis Personae*.

(a) Octavius Caesar

Octavius is the first of the minor characters in the *Dramatis Personae*. He was the nephew of Caesar and one of the Triumvirate who divided Caesar's empire among themselves. Plutarch, in his *Life of Antonius* gives an account of it:

> ...and thereupon, all three met together (to wit, Caesar, Antonius and Lepidus) in an island environed round about with a little river and there remained three days together. Now as touching all matters they were easily

> agreed and did divide all the empire of Caesar between them, as if it had been their own inheritance.[1]

According to Plutarch, it was at this time that they made a list of those men whom they condemned to death and the scene in which we see Octavius the first time is the one in which this list has been prepared. All three of them are shown as being quite ruthless in their thirst for power and Octavius follows Antony's lead in making a scapegoat of Lepidus though at first, he tries to speak for Lepidus, praising his loyalty and valour:

> You may do your will;
> But he's a tried and valiant soldier.[2]

In the end, however, he is persuaded by Antony to make a drudge of him, to be discarded when they do not need him any longer. Octavius is thus not only a mean opportunist, but a weak character in comparison with Antony. He is, to do justice to him, quite young at the time, being twenty-one, and would seem to be just a boy to the older men. In the parley scene, both Brutus and Cassius refer to him as such:

> Brutus: O, if thou wert the noblest of thy strain,
> Young man, thou could'st not die more honourable.
>
> Cassius: A peevish school-boy, worthless of such honour.[3]

In the parley scene, he shows himself quite capable of dealing with his elders, since he takes equal part in the entire conversation between the two enemy parties. In fact it is he who takes the most prominent part in it, speaking sixteen lines whereas Antony speaks eleven.

After this, we see him only in the last scene, entering with everyone as the conqueror. He shows himself in a generous light when he takes into his service Strato who was Brutus's servant. Moreover, he is the one who has the honour of ending the play, delivering what is in effect the epilogue. It is noticeable that Shakespeare does not give him any lines that mention the restoring of moral order in society. Instead he speaks about Brutus, and most significantly of sharing the proceeds of their triumph in the battle. The Elizabethans usually give the impression of a dignified and much needed restoration of moral order at the end of their tragedies. In *Macbeth*, for example, Malcolm says at the end of the play:

> What needful else
> That calls upon us, by grace of Grace
> We will perform in measure, time and place:
> So, thanks to all at once and to each one,
> Whom we invite to see us crown'd at Scone.[4]

Thus, instead of dwelling on the moral significance of the action like Malcolm, Octavius merely gives the word to end the battle:

> So call the field to rest, and let's away,
> To part the glories of this happy day.[5]

This presents gloating over victory and does not give the impression of the restoration of moral order and the installation of peace and security.

All in all, mingling good and evil, Shakespeare has given us a lifelike portrait of Octavius who, though a minor character and a young man, shows dignity and fully human qualities in the play.

(b) Lepidus

This character is the third one in the Triumvirate and is seen on the stage for the first time in the murder scene. He enters in Caesar's train and does not speak at all, so he is easily overlooked. The only scene in which he does speak is the first scene of Act IV in which he does not show himself in a good light. His lust for power makes him condemn his own brother to death, and that too, on condition that Antony's nephew also should die. It is a sordid business:

> Oct.: Your brother too must die; consent you, Lepidus?
> Lep.: I do consent—
> Oct.: Prick him down, Antony.
> Lep.: Upon condition that Publius shall not live,
> Who is your sister's son, Mark Antony.
> Ant.: He shall not live. Look, with a spot I damn him.[6]

Then he is sent away on a pretext by Antony and is not seen again in the play. Antony describes him to Octavius in most unfavourable terms, which also highlight his own cynicism and ruthlessness:

> This is a slight unmeritable man,
> Meet to be sent on such errands.
> ... ...
> Though we lay these honours on this man,
> To case ourselves of diverse sland'rous loads,
> He shall but bear them as the ass bears gold,
> To groan and sweat under the business.[7]

The dialogue goes on and Antony clarifies that he will use Lepidus only as a tool and then cast him off. Lepidus leaves the impression of being a weak and rather stupid man, morally as unscrupulous as his two cotriumvers. He is not at all a match for Antony.

(c) Cicero, Publius, Popilius Lena

These three are bracketed together as Senators. Of the three, Cicero is the most important, as he speaks the most. He is present on the stage in Act I, sc. ii, but does not speak. He converses with Casca in the next scene, only for eight-and-a-half lines. He serves as a prop for Casca in this scene, for it is to him that Casca describes the ominous portents he had seen. Cicero's comments on them mark him out as a man of sound and independent judgement:

> Men may construe things, after their fashion,
> Clean from the purpose of the things themselves.[8]

The other two hardly speak. Popilius Lena speaks just one and a half lines to Casca, showing that he is aware of their plan. It has been mentioned by Plutarch.

(d) The Conspirators—Casca

Besides Brutus and Cassius, the six conspirators are Casca, Trebonius, Ligarius, Decius Brutus, Metellus Cimber and Cinna. The first two have already been discussed earlier (*vide* Ch. 7, *supra*). It is a well-known fact that the names of all the conspirators are not given by Plutarch. He mentions Brutus, Cassius and Ligarius. Other historians mention a few other names.

Casca is the one who is next in importance to Cassius. He is the one who tells Brutus and Cassius the story of how Caesar had been presented with a crown and the manner in which he had refused it. He is presented as a cynical observer, a "blunt fellow", talking in a "sour fashion". He has noticed that Caesar refused the crown unwillingly:

> ...he put it by thrice, every time gentler than the other... to my thinking, he was very loath to lay his fingers off it.[9]

Then Brutus asks him to describe the event more in detail and Casca does so, emphasizing the unwillingness of Caesar. Then he also describes how Caesar had an epileptic fit and a few more details and then he goes away. Here, he carries out the function of reporting events that had happened off-stage.

In the second scene, we see more of him and come to know his nature better. It is a stormy night, and instead of staying at home he has come out in the violently raging storm. He has seen ominous signs:

> But never till to-night, never till now,
> Did I go through a tempest dropping fire.[10]

He goes on to tell Cicero about the fearsome portents he saw (*vide* Ch. 9, the section on Supernatural Elements, *infra*). Cicero does not attach much importance to them and it is Cassius (who comes in after Cicero has gone) who interprets them. For Cassius they all point to Caesar who, while a mere ordinary human being, is seeking to rule over other human beings. It is in the course of this dialogue that Casca joins the conspiracy:

> Hold, my hand:
> Be factious, for redress of all these griefs,
> And I will set this foot of mine as far
> As who goes furthest.[11]

His opinion of Brutus, given towards the end, is significant:

O, he sits high in all the people's hearts:
And that which would appear offence in us,
His countenance, like richest alchemy,
Will change to virtue and to worthiness.[12]

This shows a shrewd evaluation of Brutus's nobility and, in contrast, the mentality of others.

He appears thrice more, once just before Caesar sets out for the Senate and in the murder scene, in both of which he hardly speaks. He takes a more prominent part in the conspiracy scene, speaking quite a few times, though he speaks but little every time. The passage about sunrise is famous.

(e) The Conspirators—Ligarius

Ligarius is the conspirator who through pure accident and not deliberately, prevents Brutus from confiding in Portia. In Act II, sc. i Brutus is just going to tell her about the conspiracy when Ligarius knocks at the door and Brutus sends her in with the assurance that he will tell her everything. Then Ligarius comes in. He has not been keeping well and had not been able to attend the meeting of the conspirators. One of the customs of the time was for a sick man to tie a kerchief or a scarf round his head, and Ligarius, has one. This is the first thing noticed by Brutus and he voices his dismay. At once Ligarius declares that his illness will not matter if something important is to be done:

I am not sick if Brutus have in hand
Any exploit worthy the name of honour.[13]

Brutus is relieved to hear this and tells him that he has exactly such a project in mind. Ligarius says in reply:

By all the gods that Romans bow before,
I here discard my sickness. Soul of Rome!
Brave son, deriv'd from honourable loins![14]

He asks what it is that has to be done and Brutus tells him that he will explain everything as they go to meet the one "to whom it must be done". This is because it is already morning and they are going to meet Caesar. Ligarius once more declares his readiness to do whatever Brutus asks him to do and they set out for Caesar's house.

Ligarius is seen in this last part of the conspiracy scene and in the next scene, when he enters the house of Caesar along with Brutus and the other conspirators. In that scene, he is just present on the stage and does not speak. In fact he speaks only in this scene. He speaks only fourteen lines here but he gains importance because Brutus has a scene alone with him. In these 14 lines, Shakespeare has given the impression of an honourable man who has implicit faith in Brutus' honour. He is also witty, as is clear from the following terse exchange:

Brutus: A piece of work that will make sick men whole.

Caius: But are not some whole that we must make sick?[15]

In this line, with exemplary economy, Shakespeare makes clear that (a) he is witty, (b) he is aware of the conspiracy, and (c) he too agrees whole-heartedly with Brutus. It is but rarely that so much is achieved in just one line. Shakespeare has drawn Ligarius most credibly as an honest and witty man who is alive to every issue in spite of his illness. He is not mentioned in the murder scene which is, most probably, an inadvertent omission.

(f) Artemidorus

This character, designated as a Sophist, has a scene entirely to himself (Act II, sc. iii). He wants to warn Caesar against the conspirators and has written out a letter on a piece of paper, containing the names of all the conspirators. The scene he appears in is the shortest scene in the play and has been called a buffer scene (*vide* Ch. 5 *supra*). The incident of his handing the letter to Caesar has been mentioned by Plutarch:

> He marking howe Caesar received all the supplications that were offered him, and that he gave them straight to his men that were about him, pressed nearer to him, and sayed: Caesar, read this memorial to yourself and that quickly, for they be matters of great waight and touch you neerely.[16]

Caesar, however, does not read it there. Neither he nor anyone else know what is in the paper; they all take it for a petition and therefore neglect it. So Artemidorus's warning goes in vain.

(g) Lucilius

Lucilius shows himself to be a loyal friend of Brutus. He is designated as one of the friends of Brutus and is seen in Act IV, sc. ii. He had gone on an official visit to Cassius and comes back and reports to Brutus. After this, he hardly speaks, but proclaims himself to be Brutus, thus hoping to save the real Brutus:

Luc.: And I am Brutus, Marcus Brutus, I!
Brutus, my country's friend: know me for Brutus![17]

The soldiers, who do not know Brutus, take him prisoner. Then Antony comes. Lucilius makes it clear to Antony that he is willing to give himself up in order to save Brutus:

Safe, Antony; Brutus is safe enough
I dare assure thee that no enemy
Shall ever take alive the noble Brutus.[18]

He shows himself to be a real friend of Brutus, loyal even unto death. This story is given by Plutarch in his life of Brutus. Actually, Lucilius had not been put to death, but Shakespeare does not say anything about that, beyond making it clear that Antony receives him like a friend.

(h) Titinius

Titinius, like Lucilius, is a friend of Brutus and Cassius. He comes into prominence in Act V, sc. iii, one of the battle-scenes. Cassius is discussing the strategies of the battle with him when he (Cassius) suddenly sees his own tents to be on fire. He sends Titinius out to find out what has really happened. Then Pindarus reports that Titinius has been taken prisoner and Cassius commits suicide. Directly afterwards Titinius enters with Messala to bring Cassius the news that Brutus's army has triumphed over that of Octavius when they find his dead body. How deeply Titinius loved Cassius becomes clear in his eloquent grief:

But Cassius is no more. O setting sun,
As in thy red rays thou dost sink tonight,

So in his red blood Cassius day is set.

The sun of Rome is set. Our day is gone.[19]

Then he sends Messala off to take the news to Brutus and in a few moving lines, expresses his love for Cassius and grief for his death. He puts a wreath of victory sent by Brutus round his brow and then kills himself:

Brutus, come apace,
And see how I regarded Caius Cassius.
By your leave, gods. This is a Roman's part:
Come, Cassius sword, and find Titinius heart.[20]

Titinius loved Cassius so much that he could not bear the thought of living without him, all alone. It is clear that his death is far more noble and glorious than that of Cassius. Cassius died in the belief that they had lost the battle and also because he saw Titinius being taken prisoner. Titinius, however, dies only because of Cassius, though he was sure that they had won the battle. He gives his life for friendship's sake. Like Lucilius, he too leaves an impression of nobility and loyalty. Both of them are ideal examples of Shakespeare's art of portraying minor characters, though they come for a short time only.

(i) The Poet (Phaonius)

There are two poets in this play, Cinna the Poet killed by the mob and another Poet (not named) who comes in briefly in the quarrelling scene. The incident has been described by Plutarch who also gives his name. Phaonius came into Brutus's tent and recited two lines from *The Iliad*:

> This Phaonius at that time, in despite of the doorkeepers, came into the chamber and...he rehearsed the verses which old Nestor says:
>
> My lords, I pray you, harken both to mee,
> For I have seen moe years than suchye three.
>
> Cassius fel a laughing at him: but Brutus thrust him out of the chamber, and called him dogge.[21]

Referring to this incident, Shaw has made a remark that is characteristic of his attitude to the play:

> If Shakespeare had been able to present his play to the ghost of the great Julius, he could probably have had much the same reception.[22]

Besides these, there are many other male minor characters who, though individualized, need not be discussed separately. There are thirty-seven minor characters, excluding the Ghost.

(j) Calpurnia

Calpurnia, Caesar's wife, appears in two scenes only. In the first of them (Act I, sc. ii) she appears in Caesar's train and speaks only two words. In the second (Act II, sc. ii) which is located in Caesar's house she shows a natural wifely solicitude for her husband. A storm has been raging all night and still continues in the morning and she does not want Caesar to leave the house. Besides, she has had dreams with awful portents. She has also heard of dangerous omens from others and is frightened. It is here that, trying to make Caesar stay at home, she says the well-known lines about signs and portents:

> When beggars die, there are no comets seen;
> The heavens themselves blaze forth the death of princes.[23]

When Caesar is adamant in his resolution, she still does not give up trying to hold him back. She falls upon her knees and begs him not to go:

> Alas, my lord,
> Your wisdom is consum'd in confidence.
> Do not go forth to-day: call it my fear
> That keeps you in the house, and not your own.[24]

The second line in the passage quoted above contains a bitter truth: that Caesar is over-confident. His pride has overcome his wisdom, and who would know this better than his wife? Her terrible dreams, given in graphic detail, have shaken her and this is all the more important as she was not much given to this kind of fear. All this is given by Plutarch who also mentions that Caesar was very much perturbed by Calpurnia's dreams and her attempts to hold him back:

> Insomuch that Caesar rising in the morning, she prayed him if it were possible, not to goe out of the dores that day.... Thereby it seemed that Caesar likewise did feare

> and suspect somewhat, because his wife Calpurnia until that time was never given to any feare or supersticion.[25]

When Decius Brutus comes in, however and interprets her dreams she knows it is useless and wisely enough does not say anything more. Shakespeare has given her some good lines to deliver and has endowed her with a definite personality. She has been portrayed as a good wife, whose duty is to look after her husband, to save him from danger if possible. Unfortunately, her attempts go in vain.

(k) Portia

Portia is the second female character in this male dominated play. She is a person truly worthy of respect. She is shown as a devoted wife and an extremely strong-minded lady. Shakespeare has followed Plutarch quite closely in portraying her.

She makes her first appearance at the end of the conspiracy-scene. She has seen that Brutus has been very absent-minded and perturbed and wants to know the cause for this. In order to inspire her husband with confidence that she will not, like many other women, betray his secrets to others, she had given herself "a violent wound". Plutarch describes it:

> ...because she woulde not aske her husbande what he ailed before she had made some proofe by her selfe, she took a little razor... gave herself a great gashe with all in her thigh, that she was straight all of a gore bloode, and in continentlie after, a vehement fever tooke her.[26]

It is noticeable that Brutus gives her her due, treating her not only with great love but with respect, asking the gods to make him worthy of "this noble wife".

Two scenes later, she is seen again (Act II, sc. iv). In this scene, she is the dominating figure. Brutus has gone to meet Caesar and Portia is very anxious about him. This also has been described in detail by Plutarch. She was physically very weak at this time and could hardly stand. She sent message after message to Brutus to find out what has happened. In this scene, Shakespeare has shown the same thing. She sends Lucius to find out what was happening but before Lucius could go the

Soothsayer comes in. He, however, cannot give her any news and she sends Lucius. Plutarch recounts how she fainted because of her seakness and had to be carried into the house.

She is not seen after this scene. Her death is reported in the quarrelling scene. It is reported twice. The first time is when Brutus tells Cassius that she "swallowed fire" and died, and the second time Messala tells Brutus who pretends as if he did not know of it already. (*vide* Ch. 5, *supra*, discussion of the quarrelling scene). She has been portrayed as given by Plutarch—as a virtuous loving and extremely strong-minded lady. She is a highly individual character. The loving relationship between her and Brutus has been repeatedly remarked on. G. Wilson Knight also points out Portia's knowledge of Brutus's nature and how she adjusts herself:

> "Honour" is so strong in Brutus that Portia knows she must play to it, showing herself courageous, possessing a sense of honour.[27]

There are some more minor characters in the play who have not been discussed here. As has been pointed out already, there are thirty-seven characters in the play excluding the Ghost of Julius Caesar, and it is not possible to discuss each one of them. Flavius and Marullus, though they take prominent parts in the opening scene, are not seen again. Cinna the Poet comes in just one scene. There are also the two servants Lucius (servant to Brutus) and Pindarus (servant to Cassius) and the Soothsayer who are all sketched in with care though they are minor persons and do not speak much in the play. Talking about the art of characterization in *Julius Caesar* in particular, Bullough has pointed out Shakespeare's indebtedness to Plutarch:

> What Shakespeare learnt from clearly than before the paradoxes of human nature, the mixture of good and evil in the same person.[28]

NOTES

1. Plutarch's *Life of Antonius*, cited in Dorsch, *op. cit.*, p. 155.
2. Act IV, sc. i, ll. 27-28, p. 93.
3. Act V, sc. i, ll. 59-61, p. 116.

4. Macbeth, Act V, sc. vii, ll. 101-04, in Craig, W.J. ed., *The Complete Works of Shakespeare*, London, Oxford Univ. Press.
5. Act V, sc. v, ll. 80-81, p. 130.
6. Act IV, sc. i, ll. 2-6, p. 91.
7. Act IV, sc. i, ll. 12-22, p. 92.
8. Act I, sc. iii, ll. 34-35, p. 26.
9. Act I, sc. ii, ll. 225-38, pp. 19-20.
10. Act I, sc. iii, ll. 9-10, p. 24.
11. Act I, sc. iii, ll. 117-20, p. 30.
12. Act I, sc. iii, ll. 157-60, p. 32.
13. Act II, sc. i, ll. 316-17, p. 49.
14. Act II, sc. i, ll. 320-21, pp. 49-50.
15. Act II, sc. i, ll. 327-28, p. 50.
16. Bullough, *op. cit.*, p. 85.
17. Act V, sc. iv, ll. 7-8, pp. 124-25.
18. Act V, sc iv, ll. 20-22, p. 125.
19. Act V, sc. iii, ll. 60-63, p. 122.
20. Act V, sc. iii, ll. 87-90, pp. 122-23.
21. Bullough, *op. cit.*, p. 114.
22. Ure, *op. cit.*, p. 41.
23. Act II, sc. ii, ll. 30-31, p. 52.
24. Act II, sc. ii, ll. 48-51, p. 54.
25. Bullough, *op. cit.*, pp. 83-84.
26. *Ibid.*, p. 98.
27. Ure, *op. cit.*, p. 141.
28. Bullough, *op. cit.*, p. 57.

8

The Plot Structure

Though Shakespeare did not adhere strictly to the classical rules of drama, yet, he was no slip-shod craftsman. Even in early works like *Love's Labour's Lost* and *Comedy of Errors* he, keeping in mind the tricky relationship between plot and character, chooses his characters in such a way as to have a neat plot. Plot is the first and the most important element, according to Aristotle, in drama. He of course, talks about tragedy but the rules are applicable to all kinds of plays. *Julius Caesar*, though it is historical, yet is primarily a tragedy and the rules given by him are definitely applicable to it. Some of the basic rules shall now be outlined, and their applicability to *Julius Caesar*.

The Classical Rules and Julius Caesar

The Unities: These are the rules that are the most familiar with the classical rules concerning plot. Aristotle has called the plot the very basic element of drama.

> The Plot, then, is the first principle, and, as it were, the soul of a tragedy.[1]

If the plot is the first principle of a tragedy, then the theory of unities is the first principle of plots. Aristotle talks mainly of the unity of action, not so much about the unity of time and of place. It was due to a too enthusiastic interpretation of Aristotle by the Italian critics of the Renaissance, like Scaliger, Minturno, Castelvetro and others that the unity of place came to be regarded as one of the Aristotelian unities. Among the Elizabethans, Ben Jonson was the one and the only dramatist to observe all the classical rules including the unities. Shakespeare had a sovereign disregard for them, though in *The Tempest* he showed that he could easily observe them if he had a mind to it. Pope, for that matter, holds it impractical to judge him by classical rules and declares in no uncertain terms:

> To judge therefore of Shakespeare by Aristotle's rules, is like trying a man by the laws of one country, who acted under those of another. He writ to the people and writ at first...without that knowledge of the models, the ancients, to inspire him with an emulation of them.[2]

(a) *The Unity of Action*: Aristotle makes it clear that there should not be any mingling of serious actions with comic ones. This rule is especially important for tragedies and as such, can be applied to our play. The action of *Julius Caesar* can be said to be uniformly serious. The nearest approach to comic relief is to be found in the quarrel scene when the poet Phaonius comes in and exhorts Cassius and Brutus to desist from quarrelling. Plutarch says with reference to this incident that Cassius started to laugh at the poet though Brutus did not, and thrust him out of the tent. (*Vide* Ch. 8, the character of the Poet, *supra*).

(b) *The Unity of Time*: Aristotle holds that the action of a play should cover the time-span of "a single revolution of the sun", that is, a full day. Ideally (which is almost, but not absolutely impossible) the action of a play should cover only as much time as taken by the actual performance. That is, if the play takes two hours on the stage to perform, then the actual time taken by the story of the play should also take only two hours. The tragedies which Aristotle knew about, classical tragedies, fulfilled this virtually impossible requirement. Aristotle has extended the time limit to one full day and Ben Jonson's plays fulfill this requirement.

Such a time-scheme however, is not possible to observe in all kinds of plays—the chronicle plays, for example. Shakespeare hardly ever observes this rule (except in *The Tempest*). The most well-known exception to this rule occurs in *The Winter's Tale*, in which there is a gap of sixteen years within the play. So far as our play is concerned, the play begins on the day of the Lupercalia, that is, on 15th February, 44 B.C., and the battle of Philippi ended in 42 B.C. So the play covers nearly two years. This kind of compression of time is inevitable in all history plays, which, after all, *Julius Caesar* is.

(c) *The Unity of Place*: This rule demands that there should be no changes of scenes in a play. The action should take place in one place only. Sophocles's *Oedipus Rex*, for example, takes place in the throne-room of the king. Ben Jonson, though he follows this rule, still gives a few changes of scenes, but Shakespeare had not paid it much attention. He covers, not only different places in the same city, but spreads over different countries. Neo-classical critics had severely criticized him for the violation of this rule, but Dr. Johnson's defence of him has become famous. In *Julius Caesar* also, there are many changes of scenes. The first half of the play takes place in Rome, though with many changes of locations. After that, for two scenes the location shifts to Sardis, and the last Act takes place at Philippi.

Many other rules about plot had been formulated by Aristotle. European commentators, especially those of the Italian Renaissance, explained and extended them. Latin works were very popular in Elizabethan England. One such writer was Donatus, whose treatise on Dramas was part of the school curriculum. He, following Aristotle, has divided the progress of action into five parts. His divison is a little different from that of Aristotle, but, being more adaptable, became accepted and gained popularity. The prologue begins the action, as indeed, it does with the old classical plays of Aristotle's time also. It is a short speech, coming before the actual action begins, telling the reader about the theme and the story of the play. Several plays of Shakespeare have such a prologue attached to them. Usually, however, the prologue is incorporated within the first scene of the first Act. This is the case with the present play as well. It does not have a prologue. Instead there is the scene in the market-place which acquaints the audience with the prevailing situation.

Apart from these, there were certain other features of the plot that the Elizabethans knew and employed in their plays.

One such device is "Peripeteia" or reversal of fortunes. This term is usually used with reference to tragic heroes whose fortunes undergo a change for the worse, and therefore, it has negative associations. Ernest Schanzer, analyzing the play as a Problem Play, focuses upon Brutus's actions. Brutus by making the wrong choice, though from the noblest of motives, has brought about only destruction and chaos in his country. This is a reversal of fortune or *peripeteia*. Then Schanzer mentions how Brutus is told about the death of seventy senators by proscription as well as the terrible suicide of Portia. Schanzer remarks:

> The two elements which Aristotle thought necessary for the profoundest tragedy, peripeteia and anagnorisis, an ironic turn of events which make an action have the very opposite effect of that intended and the realization of this by the agent, are thus seen to be fundamental to our play.[3]

Everyone may not agree with this view and the second of the two terms used needs explanation. *Anagnorisis* is another important element of the plot, though it is concerned vitally with characters. It can be of a very elementary kind as when characters who have been separated meet and recognize each other. The Recognition-scene in *Twelfth Night* is an example of this kind of recognition. The most subtle kind of recognition is self-recognition, in which as character is able to recognize the complexities hidden within himself. This is the kind of *anagnorisis* which, according to the critic quoted above, we find in *Julius Caesar*. But everyone does not agree with this view, Virgil K. Whitaker, for example, thinks that this element, or something like it, is lacking in the play. He does not use the term *anagnorisis* or recognition. Instead, he explains that usually towards the end, the hero realizes the mistake he had made:

> Every hero except Brutus recognizes and states explicitly the full extent of his error.[4]

Whitaker calls this feature "self-revelation", but it can also be called *anagnorisis*.

Certain Elizabethan Features

One of the requisites for a tragedy, according to the Aristotelian rules, is that there should be but one plot in a tragedy. Intrigues are expected, but a fully developed sub-plot is against the rules. They are permitted in comedies, especially in the New Comedies, but not in tragedies. Elizabethan tragedies have this special feature that they often have more than one plot. Multiplicity of plots is a notable feature in Elizabethan plays as also is the use of disguises. Both of these can be omitted from this discussion as they do not occur in the play that is being studied. The action of *Julius Caesar* as will be pointed out in the relevant section, is known for its simplicity.

One of the important features of Elizabethan plays is the soliloquy. They are speeches delivered by a character when he is alone on the stage. They deal with the speaker's thoughts. The character may tell us what he is going to do in future, he may tell us about his impression of events that have happened, etc. They are like talking aloud. So far as *Julius Caesar* is concerned, it is remarkable how few soliloquies are there in it. There are, in all, only six soliloquies in it and three of them are not important ones:

1. Cassius' soliloquy: Act I, sc. ii, ll. 305-19, p. 23.
2. Brutus's: Act II, sc. i, ll. 10-33, 44-58, 61-69, 77-85, pp. 33-39.
3. Artemidorus's: Act II, sc. iii, ll. 1-14, p. 58.
4. Antony's: Act III, sc. i, ll. 254-75, pp. 76-77.
5. Brutus's: Act IV, sc. iii, ll. 266-73, p. 111.
6. Titinius's: Act V, sc. iii, ll. 80-90, pp. 122-23.

Of these, nos. 3, 5, and 6 are not important. No. 3 is the one delivered by Artemidorus resolving to hand his warning in the form of a letter to Brutus. The fifth is Brutus's short soliloquy just before the appearance of the Ghost. The last is Titinius's soliloquy before he commits suicide. He is one of the minor characters in the army of Cassius and kills himself on seeing his dear friend Cassius's dead body. It is a noble and moving soliloquy of ten lines only.

Soliloquies 1, 2, and 4 are very important ones from the point of view of character as well as plot. Virgil K. Whitaker, who interprets the play as a continuation of the morality play tradition, gives them great importance:

> The interpretation of the play as a whole turns upon the three key soliloquies by Cassius, Brutus and Antony.[5]

These three soliloquies have been interpreted and analyzed in different ways by different critics. The first of these is Cassius's soliloquy at the end of the second scene of Act I. Brutus has just left him after promising to meet him later. He shows a shrewd understanding of Brutus's character:

> Well, Brutus, thou art noble; yet I see
> Thy honourable mettle may be wrought
> From that it is dispos'd.[6]

Cassius realizes that he has made Brutus face the classic ethical problem: whether the end (ending of tyranny) justifies the means (murder of Caesar), and that Brutus is likely to join them. It is his nobility and patriotism and idealism which will make him join them. Traversi has remarked in this connection:

> The observation amounts finally to a confession of political cynicism.[7]

Even if that is true, this soliloquy reveals Brutus's character and Cassius's understanding of it. It also takes the play a step forward as Cassius is more or less sure of Brutus's decision. He, moreover, tells us in this soliloquy that he will scatter messages all over Brutus's house that will help him to make up his mind by appealing to his patriotism and subtly flattering him. He ends the soliloquy with a Senecan couplet:

> And after this, let Caesar seat him sure,
> For we will shake him, or worse days endure.[8]

The next important soliloquy, easily, the most important of all, is Brutus's soliloquy in his orchard. Almost every critic has been puzzled and intrigued by it. It contains several anomalies, though it seems to follow a logical pattern. It is a very long soliloquy, though with several breaks (three to be exact) and comes in four separate units. It should, however, be treated as one. It is particularly with reference to this soliloquy that L.C. Knights has observed:

> It is a principle of Shakespearean, indeed of Elizabethan stage-craft that when a character, in soliloquy or otherwise, develops a line of argument...we are expected to follow the argument with some attention.[9]

Brutus begins by saying that Caesar must be killed, that is, the murder is seen to be a foregone conclusion. Then he sets out to justify the murder and reconciles it with his conscience. He says he has no personal issues:

> I know no personal cause to spurn at him,
> But for the general.[10]

Then he goes on to say that if and when Caesar is crowned, his nature might change. He is almost sure it will be a change for the worse and he will have the power to do whatever he will want. The entire argument has been summed up by Coleridge thus:

> What Brutus is really saying is that he would have no objection to a king, or to Caesar as a monarch in Rome, would Caesar but be as good a monarch as he now seems disposed to be.[11]

Thus the soliloquy goes on, interrupted no less than three times. During the course of it, Brutus also reads one of the anonymous notes scattered in his house by Cassius, exhorting him to wake up and take up a stand against tyranny. By this time his mind is made up. It is in this soliloquy that those famous lines occur:

> Between the acting of a dreadful thing
> And the first motion, all the interim is
> Like a phantasma, or a hideous dream.[12]

These lines are preceded by the information that he has not been able to sleep after his talk with Cassius. All this shows the deeply perturbed condition of his mind. Dowden has called this soliloquy:

> ...an excellent example of the peculiar brooding or dwelling style which Shakespeare appropriated to the soliloquies of men.[13]

Many critics have found this soliloquy to be a succession of many stages of self-deception. However, it is a crucial soliloquy, showing the making of a moral choice which will influence not only the play but the future history of a whole nation. Virgil K. Whitaker has compared it with Dr. Faustus's opening soliloquy in which he decides to give up academic learning and pursue forbidden knowledge. There too, the moral choice made is a wrong one, leading to the eventual damnation of Faustus. Here, the question is not a religious or a spiritual one, but, looking at the plot, it is a disastrous choice. Hereby, it has been pointed out by the same critic that the device of soliloquy has gained a new importance in this play, for it influences the structure.

The supernatural plays a very important role in Elizabethan plays. So far as Shakespeare's plays are concerned, he has made repeated use of the supernatural element. In *A_Midsummer Night's Dream*, and *The Tempest*, supernatural characters take an active part in the action. These are exceptions, but in other plays also supernatural characters indirectly influence the action as the three Witches in *Macbeth* and the Ghost in *Hamlet* do. In this play, the influence exercised by supernatural elements is even less direct, but yet it exists. As a matter of fact, the different supernatural elements do not influence the action so much as create an atmosphere of ominous disaster. The Ghost of Julius Caesar, of course, is the most important of them, for he can be called a character. The rest are all signs and omens.

A most pertinent and revealing remark has been made about the Ghost by Bullough:

> By transforming Brutus's "evil spirit" or genius into Caesar's ghost, Shakespeare makes the Battle of Philippi a personal triumph for the dead man as well as his avengers.[14]

Though the Ghost appears twice to Brutus, it appears only once on the stage, in Act IV, sc. iii. This is the scene in which Brutus and Cassius quarrel, then Titinius and Messala come and there is a planning out of the morrow's battle strategy. By the time everyone is gone, Brutus is physically and mentally exhausted and wants only to rest. It is then that the Ghost appears.

At first, Brutus thinks it to be a hallucination and then starts questioning it as to its nature:

> Art thou any thing?
> Art thou some god, some angel, or some devil
> That mak'st my blood cold and my hair to stare?[15]

In reply, he hears the ominous words "Thy evil spirit, Brutus". Then in answer to the question as to why it has come it says: "To tell thee thou shalt see me at Philippi". It once more repeats the words "Ay, at Philippi" and then vanishes. In all, it barely speaks two lines, numbering ten words. In comparison with two other Shakespearean ghosts, that of Banquo first, at least it speaks, however briefly, whereas Banquo's Ghost does not speak at all. Secondly, in comparison with the Ghost of the elder Hamlet, it speaks very little. What it does say is nothing new, as the information given by Hamlet's Ghost are. As A.C. Bradley has remarked:

> Caesar's Ghost says nothing that Brutus's own forebodings might not have conjured up.[16]

As has already been observed, this Ghost does not influence the action, but acts as an ominous portent.

Another significant purpose served by the Ghost is that it provides the element of Spectacle (*opsis*) as required by the Aristotelian rules. Spectacle is one of the six elements of drama as given by him. In this case, moreover, as it is a supernatural element, and not a man-made spectacle like a pageant or a masque, it is the element of the wonderful or the Marvellous that is so often present in drama. Aristotle says:

> The element of the wonderful is required in Tragedy.... The poet should prefer probable impossibilities to improbable possibilities. The tragic plot must not be composed of irrational parts.... But once the irrational has been introduced and an air of likelihood imparted to it, we must accept it.[17]

The Ghost thus fulfills the requirement of "the wonderful" which is a must in tragedy. It is something which is definitely irrational, but, then, Shakespeare introduces it in a rational manner by first making Brutus doubt it and then accept it. So it comes within the sphere of "probable impossibility" allowed by Aristotle.

The other supernatural manifestations are all reported by eye-witnesses, not presented on the stage. Thus they cannot be included within the category of Spectacle. They start with Casca's report of the portents he has seen in Act I, sc. iii. He reports four such omens: the slave whose hand burnt without hurting him, a lion he saw in the Capitol, a hundred women who saw men all a-ire walking, an owl hooting in the market-place at noon. Of these, Plutarch mentions the first and the last as well as men on fire walking about.

The next report on supernatural elements is given by Calpurnia in Act II, sc. ii. She tells of a lioness bringing forth her young on the street, of graves opening and ghosts coming out of them, of fiery soldiers fighting in the sky, of ghosts shrieking in the streets. This last phenomenon has been mentioned in *Hamlet*. Calpurnia's descriptions are graphic and awe-inspiring:

> A lioness hath whelped in the streets,
> And graves have yawn'd and yielded up their dead;
> Fierce fiery warriors fight upon the clouds
> . . .   .
> And ghosts did shriek and squeal about the streets.[18]

It is true that these are just recounted, not shown, but so vivid is the description, that they seem to be in front of the reader.

The fact that the beast sacrificed by the priest did not have a heart, has also been listed by Plutarch among the portents seen before Caesar's death. Then comes the account of Calpurnia's ominous dream:

> She dreamt to-night she saw my statue,
> Which like a fountain with an hundred spouts
> Did run pure blood; and many lusty Romans
> Came smiling and did bathe their hands in it
> And these does she apply for warnings and portents.[19]

This presages the blood-bath which is going to really take place after the assassination. Calpurnia's dream is given by Plutarch, but not in such detail and in a different manner. He just says:

> For she dreamed that Caesar was slaine and that she had him in her armes.[20]

Later, however, Plutarch reports how Pompey's statue ran blood at Caesar's death. This is the detail given by Shakespeare, with modifications, as a dream to Calpurnia. It is most effective, as it anticipates what really happened after Caesar's death. Traversi says:

> Calpurnia's dream answers to the elemental disturbances already described at length. It forms an extension of the play's emotional climate.[21]

This is by no means the end of the supernatural portents in the play. Some more are described by Cassius just before the Battle of Philippi. When he was coming from Sardis, two eagles perched on "the foremost ensigns" and accompanied them to the battle-field. But then they went away:

> This morn are they fled away and gone,
> And in their steads do ravens, crows and kites
> Fly o'er our heads.[22]

All these omens serve to create an atmosphere of impending disaster in the play and they have been mentioned by Plutarch. It is true that they are all reported phenomena, but that does not take away their effect.

The Sources of *Julius Caesar*

The Elizabethan dramatists used to take the material for their plays from many existing sources, like pre-existing plays, romances, narrative poems, histories, etc. This, indeed, used to be done in classical times also. As far as Shakespeare's plays are concerned, the study of his sources has become an established branch of literary criticism. It is an absorbing study and reveals his organizing power. He selected materials from many different sources, rejected some and retained some, elaborated some and modified some according to his needs. Verity sums up the position thus:

> His position is that of the Greek tragedians. He dealt with the existing material of drama...much as they dealt with the cycles of Greek traditional myth: and exercising the same sovereign liberty of appropriation, he turned it to the same account.[23]

As far as *Julius Caesar* is concerned, it is a well-known fact that Shakespeare had turned to Lord North's translation of Plutarch's *Lives of Noble Grecians and Romans* for his material. In addition to this, Geoffrey Bullough has given several other possible sources. Out of these, Bullough has designated some as Analogues and some as Possible Sources. The Analogues are:

1. *The Histories of Sallust*—transl. by Thomas Heywood (1608).
2. *The Roman History of Velleius Paterculus*—transl. by Sir R. Le Grys (1632).
3. *The Historie of Twelve Caesars* by Suetonius—transl. by Philemon Holland (1606).
4. *The Roman Histories of Florus*—transl. by E.M. Bolton (1619).
5. *The Governour* by Sir Thomas Elyot (1531).
6. *The Mirror for Magistrates* (1587 edn.), Caius Julius Caesar by John Higgins.
7. *Caesar Interfectus* by Richar Eedes.

The possible sources listed by Bullough are:

1. *The First Booke of the Annales of Cornelius Tacitus*— transl. by R. Grenewey (1598).
2. *The Civil Wars by Appian of Alexandria*—transl. by W.B. (1578).
3. *It Cesare* by Orlando pescetti (1594).
4. *Caesar's Revenge* by Anon. author (1607).

Out of Plutarch, he has taken three *Lives* as the main source, those of Caesar, Brutus and Cicero. Yet, it cannot be doubted that the other eleven books listed above existed for reference and Shakespeare turned to Plutarch for most of his information. He took the events from him as well as the characters. Seeing the characters with the eyes of his own creative talent, he developed them and the relationships between them. Plutarch was no superficial recorder of events, he also evaluated the characters and this is where Shakespeare is indebted to him the most:

> For what Shakespeare learned from Plutarch was to represent more clearly than before, the paradoxes of human motive, the mixture of good and evil in the same person.[24]

In the present instance, however, we are more concerned with plot than with character, and it is here that Shakespeare's genius for organization comes to the fore. He altered many details for greater dramatic effect. Right in the beginning, for example, he altered the date of Caesar's triumph. This celebration had been held in October, 45 B.C., and the Lupercalia festival with which the play opens used to take place in February. Shakespeare has made the two dates coincide for greater effect. The disrobing of Caesar's images also had happened later, and Shakespeare has brought it forward.

In the third Act also, there are many changes. There is condensation as well as expansion. Brutus had delivered two speeches and Antony's Forum speech had not been delivered on the same day as Brutus's, but on the following day. One significant change made by the poet concerns the death of Cinna the poet by mob violence. The account given by Plutarch is slightly different from how Shakespeare has put it. The incident can be taken as an example of how he makes changes for the sake of dramatic quality. Plutarch makes it clear that the mob did not know that this was a different man from Cinna the conspirator. But Shakespeare makes Cinna the poet declare that he is a poet, not the conspirator, and yet the crowd kills him:

Cinna: Truly, my name is Cinna

1 Pleb.: Tear him to pieces! He is a conspirator

Cin.: I am Cinna the poet, I am Cinna the poet

4 Pleb.: Tear him for his bad verses...

Cin.: I am not Cinna the conspirator.[25]

But the crowd kills him all the same. This highlights the unreasonable violence of the mob. There are numerous such changes made throughout the play for the sake of greater dramatic effect. Octavius whose arrival takes place in a most dramatic manner in the same scene just after the murder, actually arrived six weeks later. The Triumvirate was formed with Lepidus after a further year and half of bitterness and fighting. Shakespeare moreover gives only one battle at Philippi, whereas there had been two. Brutus refers to the second:

> 'Tis three O'clock; and Romans, yet ere night
> We shall try our fortunes in a second fight.[26]

Actually, the second fight had taken place nearly three weeks after the first. Shakespeare has brought the two together. There are many such instances of departure from his sources which have all contributed to the formation of an extremely stream-lined play, written with great economy. Traversi, indeed, has suggested three principles followed by Plutarch which influenced Shakespeare in adapting his sources. First of all, Plutarch had a genius for dramatizing his heroes. He gave his subjects set speeches of importance when dealing with moments of decision or of action. This tends to present, not just a sequence of events as history is supposed to be, but a dramatic account of it. Secondly, Plutarch always chose incidents which had dramatic possibilities in them. He recounted them in detail. This also tends to dramatization. Thirdly, Plutarch had a highly moral outlook on history. He believed that historians had the sacred duty of setting up a moral example for posterity, and chose his incidents with this view in mind (in addition to that of dramatic effect). These three features had influenced Shakespeare. He too was not content with just presenting events. His aim was different:

> It reflected deep personal meditation...upon the nature and significance of public procedures and their presentation in theatre.[27]

Shakespeare, therefore, chose to present his heroes and their actions according to his concepts of morality as well as that of theatrical effects.

The Plot of *Julius Caesar*

The plot of this play is known for its directness and simplicity. It has many episodes and intrigues, but no sub-plots. The Brutus-Cassius plot, at a superficial glance, may seem to be a sub-plot, but it is actually an intrigue. Indeed, A.C. Bradley has taken the plots of *Julius Caesar* and *Macbeth* to illustrate clear and simple plots:

> ...the tragedies in which the movement is most clear and simple. These are *Julius Caesar* and *Macbeth*.[28]

Again, comparing *Julius Caesar* with the two other plays of this trilogy, *Antony and Cleopatra* and *Coriolanus*, Traversi points out that this play:

> ...stands a little apart in this respect...we are conscious of the smooth progress of a single action and narrative current, unimpeded from the beginning of the action to its logical conclusion.[29]

As is well-known, Bradley divides the plots of Shakespearean tragedies into three parts: the exposition, the conflict and the catastrophe. Explaining the structure of *Julius Caesar* from this point of view he says that in it the conspiracy, continually facing ups and downs, rises to the climactic point in the assassination scene in Act III, sc. i. Then again, through more ups and downs, it gradually sinks down to the catastrophe, with the defeat and consequent death of Brutus and Cassius.

The exposition in this play begins with the crowd scene, at a high pitch of excitement, then sinks to the dialogue between Brutus and Cassius, which is a quite one, as Bradley points out. This is how it continues. Then in the middle section, after the crisis and before the catastrophe, there is often a falling off in pitch. Comparing *Julius Caesar* with other tragedies Bradley points out:

> *Julius Caesar, Hamlet, King Lear* and *Macbeth*, have all a tendency to "drag" in this section of the plot and that

> the first...fail(s) even in the catastrophe to reach the heart of the greatest scenes that have preceded the Fourth Act.[30]

Everyone does not agree with this view and Peter Ure calls the third Act after Caesar's death:

> ...is a most sustained and glorious piece of writing, and, in performance, enthralling.[31]

Most of the critics, however, agree that an important turning-point in the play occurs after the blood-bath. Directly after this ritual, Antony's servant enters, and it is at this point that the change in the plot comes. It has been pointed out in the most effective manner by R.G. Moulton:

> *Enter a Servant*: This simple stage-direction is the "catastrophe", the turning-point of the whole action; the arch has reached its apex and the Reaction has begun.[32]

It can thus be seen that, though *Julius Caesar* has, according to Bradley, a simple and single movement, within that itself, there is difference of opinion among the critics. A further analysis of the plot from a different point of view has been presented by Virgil K. Whitaker. He considers *Julius Caesar* as a play in the morality tradition (*vide* Ch. 4, *supra*, the section on genre). He therefore looks at the plot too from this point of view. Such plots revolve around the moral choice faced by the hero, his ultimate decision, and the result of that decision. Dr. Faustus in Marlowe's play chooses the path of evil by selling his soul to Mephistopheles, which results in the eternal damnation of his soul. When considering *Julius Caesar*, this critic calls the play "a tragedy of moral choice", and says that Shakespeare uses a definite "formula" in such plays. First of all there is the exposition in which he accomplishes three things:

(a) The dilemma facing the hero is explained, as in *Julius Caesar*.[33]

In this case, the dilemma Brutus faces is whether to kill Caesar or not.

(b) As the next step, in violation of all probability, the actual choice is made in a single scene.

(c) The false moral choice then leads to a decisive act and from that act results the hero's downfall.[34]

Usually, the hero understands the implications of the choice he has made. This is not the case with Brutus:

> Every hero except Brutus recognizes fully and states explicitly, the full extent of his error.[35]

According to Whitaker, this formula of the plot was first worked out in *Julius Caesar* and then used in his later tragedies. Plot-wise, therefore, *Julius Caesar* is something of an experiment.

E.M. Forster, delving into the reasons for the popularity of the play, points to its highly stage-worthy construction. He grants that it is not:

> Carefully constructed, like a Greek play or a classical French play, although it is not as cunning in its advance as *Othello* or *Macbeth*, yet it does succeed in starting us and holding us.[36]

According to him, the play does this "by three well-timed explosions". The first explosion is the murder of Caesar, the second, the Forum speech of Antony and the third is the quarrel between Cassius and Brutus. For him, the plot of the play thus rises to three peaks, preceded and followed by quieter scenes.

Most critics tend to divide the play into two halves, some placing the division line after Caesar's death and some before or after Antony's Forum speech. Norman Rabkin, placing the division mark after, or rather, with the speech, holds that from this point onwards the plot follows the familiar pattern of a revenge tragedy:

> Caesar is the moving force of the tragedy.
>
> The action of the play makes clear sense in terms of revenge tragedy.[37]

The audience, responding to Antony's call for revenge, expects the familiar plot of a revenge tragedy and gets it too (*vide* Ch. 4, *supra*, the section on genre). Actually the revenge motif is introduced earlier, in Antony's soliloquy over Caesar's body:

> And Caesar's spirit, ranging for revenge,
> With Ate by his side come hot from hell.[38]

A very important point has been advanced on the plot of the play by Ernest Schanzer. Laying stress upon Brutus's character, he highlights the trait of self-deception in him. He analyzes Brutus's soliloquy in the orchard and says:

> The argument is quite cogent and contains no confusions.... But it is founded on self-deception.[39]

In other words, Brutus never recognizes the fact that in choosing to kill Caesar he has made the wrong choice. This has been pointed out by Whitaker also, as has been discussed already. There is no self-recognition, or *anagnorisis* in the play. Further, from Antony's speech onwards, a turning point comes in the action as well as in the fortunes of Brutus and his fellow-conspirators. This is the beginning of *peripeteia*. Pointing out these features Schanzer remarks:

> The two elements which Aristotle thought necessary for the profoundest tragedy, peripeteia and anagnorisis, are thus seen to be fundamental to our play. They are found, in varying degrees, in all of Shakespeare's tragedies.[40]

Looking at the plot from the point of view of stage performance, Mark Hunter has given a four-fold structure of the play. It is not that he analyzes the plot in detail, he just presents the actor-manager's view:

> The varying choice of famous actor-managers...is significant.... The first Act of the tragedy is Cassius's Act, the second is Brutus's; the third is Antony's; and in the fourth and fifth Cassius and Brutus together make a joint tragic appeal.[41]

The actor-manager's view is a peculiarly relevant one, for plays, after all, are meant to be acted out on the stage, they are not meant only for the armchair analyses of the erudite scholar or the academician.

Julius Caesar thus has given rise to a multiplicity of opinions about this feature of the artistry expended on it. All these views emphasize the complexity of the play.

NOTES

1. Butcher, *op. cit.*, pp. 27-29.
2. L. Kronenberger, ed., *Alexander Pope: Selected Works*. New York, The Modern Library, 1951, pp. 353-54.
3. Ernest Schanzer, *The Tragedy of Brutus* in Ure, *op. cit.*, p. 193.
4. Virgil K. Whitaker, *op. cit.*, p. 181.
5. *Ibid.*, p. 178.
6. Act I, sc. ii, ll. 305-07, p. 23.
7. Traversi, *op. cit.*, p. 30.
8. Act I, sc. ii, ll. 318-19, p. 24.
9. L.C. Knights in Ure, *op. cit.*, p. 128.
10. Act II, sc. i, ll. 11-12, p. 34.
11. Quoted in Ure, *op. cit.*, pp. 128-29.
12. Act II, sc. i, ll. 63-65, p. 37
13. Ure, *op. cit.*, p. 34.
14. Bullough, *op. cit.*, p. 55
15. Act IV, sc.iii, ll. 277-79, p. 111
16. Bradley, *op. cit.*, p. 426.
17. Butcher, *op. cit.*, pp. 95-97.
18. Act II, sc. ii, ll. 17-24, pp. 51-52.
19. Act II, sc. ii, ll. 76-80, p. 55.
20. Bullough, *op. cit.*, p. 83.
21. Traversi, *op. cit.*, p. 41.
22. Act V, sc. i, ll. 84-86, p. 117.
23. A.W. Verity, Introduction to *Hamlet*, Cambridge, Cambridge University Press, Indian edn., 1989, pp. xx-xxi.
24. Bullough, *op. cit.*, p. 57.
25. Act III, sc. iii, ll. 27-32, p. 89.
26. Act V, sc. iii, ll. 109-10, p. 124.
27. Traversi, *op. cit.*, p. 11.
28. A.C. Bradley, *op. cit.*, p. 39.
29. Traversi, *op. cit.*, p. 10.
30. Bradley, *op. cit.*, p. 44.
31. Ure, *op. cit.*, p. 18.

32. *Ibid.*, p. 36.
33. Whitaker, *op. cit.*, p. 180.
34. *Ibid.*, p. 181.
35. *Ibid.*
36. E.M. Forster, *Julius Caesar* in Ure, p. 62.
37. Norman Rabkin, *Structure, Convention and Meaning in Julius Caesar*, in Ure, p. 105.
38. Act III, sc. i, ll. 270-71, p. 76.
39. E. Schanzer, in Ure, p. 192.
40. *Ibid.*, p. 193.
41. Mark Hunter, *Brutus and the Politic Context*, in Ure, p. 197.

9

Imagery

Imagery is an important part of poetry, especially of drama, because the images a character uses, reveal his personality, besides carrying out many other functions. Extensive as well as intensive studies of Shakespeare's imagery have been undertaken by noted scholars. The development of his imagery in the course of his career, the function of his images, the relationship between the images and the character and the theme, all these have been studied in detail. Images have been defined in many different ways. The definition given by Henri Fluchere is a very good working definition of it:

> Imagery may shortly be defined as a concrete illustration drawn upon by the poet to clarify or embellish the object that he seeks to describe.[1]

Only two functions—embellishment and clarifying, have been mentioned here. Shakespeare's imagery carries out several other functions as well, like anticipating future events, creating the atmosphere, expressing the mood of the character who is speaking. These and many other functions are carried out by images in Shakespeare.

While studying his imagery, one should not forget the fact that it is often very difficult, sometimes quite impossible, to distinguish between rhetorical figures, images and symbols. These are integrally related, often overlapping. An image is also usually a figure of speech and often it is also given the status of a symbol. Highlighting this trait, Fluchere says:

> No strict rule allows us to say at what point we pass from the plane of pure rhetoric to the plane of pure psychology, and even the metaphysical plane, in the use of imagery.[2]

Again, the same image can be considered under different heads. Thus a sense image is also a nature image or a domestic image or some such kind. This is a feature common to all images since everything is perceived through senses.

Sense-images are the most obvious kind of images. As we have five senses, these images are termed accordingly. So, corresponding to the senses of sight, hearing, smelling, tasting and touching, the images are called visual, auditory, olfactory, gustatory and tactile respectively. These will now be mentioned briefly with reference to the text. Sense images have a special feature peculiar to them only. The one and the same image may refer to several different senses. Again, the object being referred to might appeal to one of the senses, but the poet might describe it in terms of a different one. This technique is called synaesthesia.

The images that have been used in this play will now be taken up. It is not possible to study them in detail, and therefore, only a few obvious examples will be taken up to illustrate different kinds of images and the technique of using them. The longest scene in the play is the one in which the conspirators meet and decide upon their future courses of action (Act II, sc. i, 334 lines). Our examples will be taken from this scene as it gives the most scope.

It opens with a brief visual image (which is also a stellar, or an astronomical image) by Brutus:

> I cannot by the progress of the stars,
> Give guess how near to day.[3]

This is a visual image, for a star is an object that is seen (and not smelled or heard), but it is not just a simple visual image. He talks of telling the time, which is an abstract element. Thus here a concrete object has imaged forth an abstract idea. Moreover, telling the time is an intellectual activity. Thus seeing with eyes things that are concrete objects is joined with an intellectual activity. In addition, he talks of "stars" in the plural, that is, many stars are involved, which makes it a cosmic image.

In terms of sense images, those used in this scene are visual ones. There are, however, several remarkable auditory images given by Calpurnia in the next scene:

> The noise of battle hurtled in the air,
> Horses did neigh, and dying men did groan,
> And ghosts did shriek and squeal about the streets.[4]

In addition to these being sense-images of the auditory variety, there is another feature to be noted in these lines: there are five auditory images in three lines. That is, here we have an accumulation of images of the same variety. This is a feature (that is, the accumulation of images, be they of whatsoever varieties they might), in Shakespeare. In this scene also there is one such specially remarkable passage:

> That unicorns may be betrayed with trees,
> And bears with glasses, elephants with holes,
> Lions with toils, and men with flattery.[5]

Here, we have four animal images piled upon each other in only three lines. Besides being an example of accumulation of images, this passage also gives the methods of catching these animals, so these are hunting images as well.

Among animal images, two remarkable snake images have been used by Brutus in his soliloquy:

> It is the brightest day that brings forth the adder.
> . . . .
> And therefore, think him as a serpent's egg,
> Which, hatch'd, would, as his kind, grow mischievous.[6]

These two images are especially apt because they describe Brutus's idea of Caesar's ambitious nature and how he might misuse the power that royalty will bring him.

Images having to do with the vegetable world of nature, that is trees, flowers, etc. are plentiful in Shakespeare but not in this scene. They predominate in plays like *A Midsummer Night's Dream* and *As You Like It* which are pastoral in nature. Apart from this scene, they can be found in other scenes of this play, but not in any remarkable profusion. Thus, in the scene immediately preceding this one, there are a few nature images in Cassius's description of the storm which is raging that night:

I have seen tempests, when the scolding winds
Have riv'd the knotty oaks; and I have seen
Th' ambitious ocean swell and rage and foam
To be exalted with the threatening clouds.[7]

Here in the space of four lines, we have four nature images: (a) the scolding winds, (b) the riven oaks, (c) the raging ocean and (d) the threatening clouds. The poet's eyes are ranging wide—from the clouds overhead to the ocean down below and therefore take in the heavens and the earth. Also, because the images portray a storm, they are extremely dynamic. They are all mainly visual images, yet the auditory quality of the howling of the winds, the breaking of the oak and the raging of the sea can be imagined, though they have not been mentioned specially.

This does not mean that there are no nature images in this particular scene, though they are not emphatic ones. Thus when Brutus says:

It is the bright day that brings forth the adder.[8]

It is the adder that catches the reader's attention and he forgets the "bright day" which is a nature image. The line, as a matter of fact, contains two images: one a nature image and another an animal one.

Images have been taken from different spheres of life. Thus, we have an image from falconry:

So let high-sighted tyranny range on
Till each man drop by lottery.[9]

Here, "high-sounding" refers to a falcon which flies high and is also far-sighted. Likewise, some lines later, Metellus uses an image from the world of commerce:

his silver hairs
Will purpose us a good opinion,
And buy men's voices to commend our deeds.[10]

These two images make it clear that all the different phases of life have been covered by his imagery, for falconry is the pastime of the nobility and buying and selling is the work of humbler people.

A remarkable feature of Shakespeare's imagery has been noted by Caroline Spurgeon. It may so happen that there are repeated references to the same basic image like gardening, astronomy, agriculture, etc. She has called this feature "image-complex".

> The term "image-complex" is to indicate that Shakespeare, in his imagery, shows, as Miss Spurgeon has put it, a predilection for "certain classes of things, certain qualities in things and certain aspects of life".[11]

There are many such image-complexes in *Julius Caesar* and one of them occurs in this scene:

> That unicorns may be betray'd with trees,
> And bears with glasses, elephants with holes,
> Lions with toils, and men with flattery.[12]

Here, there is one all-comprehensive image of hunting, and the different methods of hunting different animals have been mentioned. Thus, there are five brief images in three lines all of which refer to the basic image of hunting.

This is undoubtedly one of the most concentrated examples of image-complexes in the whole of Shakespeare.

According to Wolfgang Clemen, there are images that serve to beautify the poetic diction in the early plays of Shakespeare, but as his art matured, gradually his images became more and more functional and integrally related to the play:

> The more Shakespeare becomes a conscious artist, the more he employs them for dramatic purposes. The images gradually lose their purely "poetic"... nature and become one of the dramatic elements.[13]

There are many such images in this scene, but the most notable of such functional images that has been singled out for illustration by Clemen occurs in sc. iii of Act I. Here, the conspirators meet on the street of Rome in a dark and stormy night. Cassius compares the terrible storm with Caesar:

Now could I, Casca, name to thee a man
Most like this dreadful night
That thunders, lightens, opens graves and roars
As doth the lion in the Capitol.[14]

This is a complex passage as far as imagery is concerned. There is the basic image of the storm raging around them. This involves auditory (thunder) and visual (lightning) as well as the macabre image of the graves opening. It also takes in the animal image of the lion. But Clemen by-passes these as being of less importance and focuses on other more important characteristics:

> The image fulfills two functions at one and the same time, it characterizes Caesar and adds to the nocturnal thunderstorm.[15]

Nearly all images carry out such functions. All the images that have been mentioned above in order to illustrate different points are also indicative of this feature,—that of being functional images illustrating moods, explaining characters, creating atmosphere, etc. One such image can be taken from this particular scene for illustration:

That lowliness is young ambition's ladder,
Where to the climber-upward turns his face;
But when he once attains the upmost round,
He then unto the ladder turns his back,
Looks in the cloud, scorning the base degrees
By which he did ascend.[16]

This elaborate image, spread over five lines can be said to carry out several functions. It highlights Brutus's contemplative and analytical mood, it explains Caesar's character and it looks back upon his past career. What is more, it forecasts the future pretty accurately, for when in the murder scene Brutus himself will kneel to Caesar in order to support Metellus's plea Caesar will refuse him. This one image thus carries out four important functions in this scene. Such examples are by no means rare.

There is a kind of image which can best be described as a hidden image. In this, the image is implied, not clearly described. Such images abound in Shakespeare. These implied or hidden images do not embellish the diction openly at all, yet they add considerably to its depth and also its far-reaching significance. There is, for example, Brutus's well-known comparison of a human being with the state:

> And the state of man,
> Like to a little kingdom, suffers then
> The nature of an insurrection.[17]

This kind of comparison of the human body with a kingdom was a very common one in all literature of the time, not just in drama. Indeed, the phrase "the body politic" is an indication of the popularity of the idea. Here Brutus is thinking, not just of any human being in general, but of his own body—at least that is what T.S. Dorsch thinks. He compares this passage with a like one in *Macbeth* and says:

> Brutus, like Macbeth, is thinking particularly of his own individual human organism; but he is also generalizing from his own experience, about the characteristic effect of a particular kind of suspense on the mind.[18]

This hidden image of the human body has intrigued other critics also, though the comparison, as has been pointed out above, is a very common one. It is with particular reference to this same passage that Traversi has observed:

> The motion that disunity in the individual is in some sense a reflection of greater cleavages, obscure rifts in the fabric of society and even, it may be, of nature itself is one which will lie very close to the heart of Shakespeare's greatest tragedies.[19]

It is, perhaps, because the image is a hidden, an implied one that it has attracted so much attention, for, as has been pointed out, it is by no means an uncommon image. The implication have added great depth to the lines.

Wolfgang Clemen has drawn attention to another feature of imagery. According to him, images can create ambiguity of meaning better than other stylistic devices, definitely better than plain diction. He has a particular kind of ambiguity in mind, though he does not specify which type it would be according to Empson, to whom he refers. He says:

> The one meaning which the speaker has in mind refers to the momentary situation, but the other meaning may point beyond this moment to other issues of the play. Imagery may serve this purpose better than plain language and may lend itself more easily to ambiguity.[20]

Then he refers specifically to Titinius's lament over the dead body of Cassius in the fifth Act. Titinius, Cassius's intimate friend, has just found his dead body and the victory which he believed they had won has become meaningless for him. It is a most eloquent and effective passage:

> O setting sun,
> As in thy red rays thou dost sink to night,
> So in his red blood Cassius's day is set.
> The sun of Rome is set. Our day is gone;
> Clouds, dews and dangers come; our deeds are done.[21]

Clemen, analyzing this passage, finds several ambiguities here. First of all, according to him, there is double meaning in the image of the setting sun, but that is just the beginning:

> The increasingly complex significance of the rest of the passage develops from the simple meaning of the first words of the sentence. The sun is doubly set, for the "sun of Rome" is both the sun of that day and Cassius himself.[22]

Then he goes on to clarify further ambiguities, for he finds no less than three meanings in the words "Our day is gone". First of all it refers to the real day which has passed with the setting of the sun. Secondly, it means Cassius and thirdly, it means the time of life that all the characters have passed through. It is perfectly true that all these meanings pass through the reader's mind as he reads the lines. What Clemen says is by no means a far-fetched idea. These ambiguities or multiple meanings do but add to the depth of the passage. He, however, does not point out that the image carries out the function of anticipating the future, though he does remark that "something new is about to begin for all of them now".

Almost all of the images studied here have been taken from just one scene, the first scene of Act II. Yet the wealth of imagery in even this one scene has barely been explored. It can be easily imagined what a treasure-house of images the entire play might be. Even the analysis of just one passage from the point of view of imagery will be very rewarding and illuminating. There are, as has been pointed out, several aspects of imagery. Apart from analyzing the several categories like sense imagery, etc., studies can be made of how they reveal the speaker's mood, create the atmosphere, anticipate the future, shed light on the theme, etc. Factors like hidden imagery, ambiguity, image-complex also should be kept in mind. Such a study of even one passage will be extremely illuminating.

NOTES

1. H. Fluchere, *op. cit.*, p. 167.
2. *Ibid.*
3. Act II, sc. i, ll. 2-3, p. 33.
4. Act II, sc. ii, ll. 22-24, p. 52
5. Act II, sc. i, ll. 204-06, p. 44.
6. Act II, sc. i, ll. 14, 32-33, pp. 34-35.
7. Act I, sc. iii, ll. 5-8, p. 24.
8. Act II, sc. i, l. 14, p. 34
9. Act II, sc. i, ll. 118-19, p. 20.
10. Act II, sc. i, ll. 144-46, p. 41.
11. Wolfgang Clemen, *The Development of Shakespeare's Imagery*, London, Methuen and Co. Ltd., 1977, p. 78.
12. Act II, sc. i, ll. 204-06, p. 44.
13. W. Clemen, *op. cit.*, p. 81.
14. Act I, sc. iii, ll. 72-75, p. 28.
15. Clemen, *op. cit.*, pp. 99-100
16. Act II, sc. i, ll. 22-27, pp. 34-35.
17. Act II, sc. i, ll. 67-69, p. 37
18. *Ibid.*, footnote.
19. Traversi, *op. cit.*, p. 36.
20. Clemen, *op. cit.*, p. 90.
21. Act V, sc. iii, ll. 60-64, p. 122.
22. Clemen, *op. cit.*, p. 90.

10

Poetic Style: Diction and Versification

Much of the success of a play depends on the poetic style used by the writer. Shakespeare's style, like all the aspects of his plays, has been studied in great detail. Several factors have to be noted here. First of all, his style has all the features of his own time, or, in other words, it is an Elizabethan style. Yet, it cannot be denied that it bears the hallmark of his own individuality. What is more, since he wrote plays, many are the persons who speak in them and the language has to be suitable for each individual character. One can only wonder at the stupendous ability of the writer in fulfilling all these requirements successfully.

Following contemporary customs, his plays were written in a mixture of prose and verse, as has been clarified earlier (*vide* Ch. 5, *supra*). The noble persons usually speak in verse and the humbler ones in prose. Exceptions are there, of course. In this play, Casca speaks in prose in the beginning, and Brutus's Forum speech in prose is a famous piece of oratory.

Poetic style has two different aspects to it. On one hand, there is diction or language and on the other, there is the technique of versification. The two aspects are distinctly different from each other and should be considered separately. First, we shall have a look at poetic diction.

(a) Poetic Diction

The classical theory of diction was a highly developed and sophisticated one. These theories were quite well-known in

Shakespeare's time, particularly the Roman ones. Horace, in his *Ars Poetica*, had laid down clear-cut rules about diction and the Elizabethan writers were familiar with them. Though there were many other theoreticians, it was Horace's theory that was the most popular.

Horace puts it down that every different form of poetry has its own particular diction, but in drama, it should be modulated according to the speaker's personality as well. The characters should speak in the kind of language that would suit their age, sex and position in society. The sentence is a famous one:

> It will make a great difference whether a God or a hero is speaking, a man of ripe years or a hot-headed youngster in the pride of youth, a woman of standing or an officious nurse, a roving, merchant or a prosperous farmer.[1]

All possibilities are covered by this sentence. First of all, divine and human characters are distinguished from each other. It is not equally easy to differentiate between characters, who, in their hundreds, crowd the world, each with his or her own distinct profession and personality. Age is an important factor, as Horace clarifies when he talks about a mature man and a younger one. Then, of course, there is great variety in each of these classes. There are so many sub-divisions according to age and social status. Horace refers to this great variety by mentioning a lady of quality as opposed to a nurse. He also differentiates between different professions by referring to an itinerary salesman and a well-established farmer. In a nutshell, then, the diction must suit every individual dramatic character. Diction, as a matter of fact, became strictly specialized in Elizabethan drama. M.C. Bradbrook has pointed this out:

> The specific style for princes, for lovers, for clowns, was fixed.[2]

Thus there are some stringent rules that the poet should always keep in mind. The diction must be natural for the speaker, and it must carry out, for the reader, two important functions, (a) it must persuade the reader or the audience, and (b) it must move him emotionally:

> The Elizabethan dramatist's style is one of impassioned poetic rhetoric, the two commonest functions of which are to persuade and to touch the emotions.[3]

The logical aspect of style and its affective aspect, both are equally important.

It is clear that, to achieve this double aim is impossible if the poet uses a plain, cut-and-dried language. He ought to make use of different rhetorical devices. Aristotle himself highlights the importance of such embellishments. The style may be the grand, or the middle or the low, depending upon the theme and the speaker, but embellishments should always be used. The main characters in, for example, Ben Jonson's *The Alchemist* belong to the lower class and in their speeches the low style is used. On the other hand, Sir Epicure Mammon, as he belongs to the nobility, speaks in the grand style. In both cases the speeches are full of figures of speech.

English critics also recommended the use of figurative language, as can be seen in the many books on rhetoric published at the time. George Puttenham in his famous *Arte of English Poesic* writes:

> There is nothing so fitte for the poem as to be furnished with all the figures that be Rhetoricall and such as do most beautifie the language with eloquence.[4]

The Greek and Latin rhetoricians have given many theories of style and its different aspects. Horace, for example, advocates the use of newly-coined words, provided they are based on Greek words and sparingly used. He also recommends the revival of words that have gone out of use, as well as of familiar language. Shakespeare not only knew all the rules and concepts prevalent in his time but made effective and continuous use of them. Yet he wrote, not by rule, but by instinct. There is never any attempt at or trying and straining for effects. Whatever style he adopts, the high, the middle or the low, everything appears perfectly natural.

(i) Diction in Julius Caesar

Shakespeare's dramatic career stretched over two decades and these years show continuous development. All the different aspects of his artistry went on developing from one play to the next. Style, imagery, plot-management, stagecraft, characterization—all went on developing even to the last play. *Julius Caesar* is a product of his mature artistry and in it he has used a diction that is eminently suited to the kind of play it is—a historical tragedy. Commenting on the poetic style of these plays, Derek Traversi observes:

> The style of these plays, far from reflecting a pedestrian process of versification, shows a unique combination of narrative lucidity, achieved through the easy, almost conversational use of speech rhythms and vernacular phrases, to poetic intensities that flow effortlessly from this foundation whenever the state of action so allows.[5]

Not only does Shakespeare use conversational rhythms and phrases and heightens it to "poetic intensities" in this and other mature plays, he adopts all the different contemporary conventions and makes them serve his purpose.

Elizabethan dramatists made use of both prose and verse and he has done the same. He uses prose and verse not merely to indicate the social position of the persons, but also in order to heighten or lower the pitch of the dialogue. Even his noble characters use prose when talking of ordinary matters, but when a loftier or more serious tone is needed they turn to poetry. This device can be applied not just to the use of prose and verse but to all kinds of style, for the diction must suit not only the character speaking, but to the situation also. In his definition of tragedy Aristotle points out that the poet must use:

> ...language enriched in a variety of ways and artistic devices appropriate to the several parts of the play.[6]

This means, in effect, that even the same character must not speak in the manner in all the different situations in the play. *Julius Caesar* is no exception to this basic rule. The difference in style is the most remarkable in Brutus. When deliberating in his own mind, as in the orchard scene, he speaks in a slow, meditative manner, using frequent conversational turns in his sentences. Speaking to the conspirators, he uses a far more formal manner. Again, when talking to Portia he speaks in tender, colloquial language. All this is changed in his Forum speech, which is a piece of splendid oratory in formal and balanced sentences. As a matter of fact, this kind of formal style is peculiarly suited to this play, which deals with Romans who took the art of rhetoric very seriously indeed. Oratory was a highly developed, sophisticated art. Emma Smith has drawn attention to this:

> *Julius Caesar* is insistently public, full of oratory and debate, and even private scenes are marked by lofty rhetoric. Rhetoric was the primary vehicle for Roman politics.[7]

Julius Caesar uses many rhetorical devices and some of them will now be discussed. Examples will be taken from Act II, sc. i as had been done with imagery in the foregoing chapter.

(ii) Stylistic Devices

Many different kinds of stylistic devices are there of which the uses of imagery, symbolism and figures of speech are the most important. Of these, imagery has already been studied in the foregoing chapter and now some of the most important figures of speech used by the poet shall be taken up.

The simile is one of the most obvious figures of speech and some of the most remarkable ones among them occur in this scene. Apart from minor ones, there are three oft-quoted very effective similes, all spoken by Brutus. The first of them occurs quite early in it:

> And therefore, think him as a serpent's egg,
> Which, hatch'd, would, as his kind, grow mischievous,
> And kill him in the shell.[8]

Here, Brutus makes use of a concrete image (a sepent's egg) in order to describe something concrete (Caesar), but in the next simile both are abstract:

> Between the acting of a dreadful thing
> And the first motion, all the interim is
> Like a phantasma, or a hideous dream.[9]

This is a remarkable simile, because here, both the initial object and that which it is compared to, are highly abstract images. Yet one experiences no difficulty in understanding the basic idea behind it all. Such a passage fully justified Traversi's remark:

> This marriage of colloquial ease with the heights of emotional experience is achieved with a consistency hardly paralleled elsewhere in Shakespeare's work.[10]

Right from the classical times, metaphors have been looked upon as a very important means for enhancing poetic effect. There are numerous metaphors in this scene, several in the first soliloquy of Brutus. The first occurs when he is thinking of crowning Caesar:

> And then, I grant, we put a sting in him,
> That at his will he may do danger with.[11]

A few lines later, in an oft-quoted passage, he makes use of the metaphor of a climber:

> That lowliness is young ambition's ladder
> Where to the climber-upward turns his face;
> But when he once attains the upmost round,
> He then unto the ladder turns his back.[12]

This particular metaphor is so effective because of many reasons. First of all, it is not just a metaphor—it involves personification also, since ambition is personified. Secondly, it is a dynamic metaphor, for it involves motion, that of climbing a ladder. Again, it also contains a certain amount of narration, for it describes not only a youth gradually climbing up, but also what he does on reaching the top. It takes in many things within its compass: the youthful figure of ambition, the inanimate object ladder and the sky to which the climber looks up, with all its manifold associations.

Just as simile and metaphor heighten the descriptive element in poetry, so does apostrophe heighten its dramatic quality. In the next part of his soliloquy, Brutus makes use of this figure of speech:

O Rome, I make thee promise,
If the redress will follow, thou receivest
Thy full petition at the hand of Brutus.[13]

Again, after two interruptions and about nine lines of soliloquy, he uses another apostrophe. The conspirators have come, and Lucius has told him that, except for Cassius, nobody else can be recognized:

O conspiracy,
Shamest thou to show thy dangerous brow by night,
When evils are most free? O, then by day
Where wilt thou find a cavern dark enough
To mask thy monstrous visage?[14]

Apart from apostrophe, rhetorical questions also lend a dramatic quality to poetry, and Shakespeare makes very effective use of this figure of speech. In the passage quoted above, for example, there are two rhetorical questions in addition to apostrophe. A succession of rhetorical questions are asked by Brutus in his speech to the conspirators:

What need we any spur but our own cause
To prick us to redress? What other bond
Than secret Romans, that have spake the word,
And will not palter? and what other oath
Than honesty to honesty engag'd,
That this shall be, or we will fall for it?[15]

Here, we have three rhetorical questions, one after the other, adding a dynamic and dramatic quality to poetry.

Just as apostrophe and rhetorical questions give a dramatic quality to poetry, so do figures of speech like epigrams, antitheses, paradoxes, etc. give a pointed and precise quality to it. An epigram occurs quite early in the scene, in Brutus's first soliloquy:

It is the bright day that brings forth the adder.[16]

Commenting on this epigram and the simile about the serpent's egg (quoted above), Derek Traversi has observed:

> It is part of the presentation of human contradiction whose exposition is so close to the spirit of the day.[17]

Epigrams are based on contradiction and it is the contrast between the bright day and the venomous adder that makes this epigram so effective.

Repetition or tautology is effectively used by poets to give expansion to their work. Shakespeare, in a certain instance, has used it to give his poetry a pointed quality in the way an epigram, for example, might do. Portia thus objects to being kept in the dark about Brutus's plans:

> I grant I am a woman, but withal
> A woman that Lord Brutus took to wife;
> I grant I am a woman, but withal
> A woman well-reputed, Cato's daughter.[18]

Here, the repetition of a whole line gives a pointed quality to the verse. This is not only because there is repetition in these lines, but because there is also anti-thesis:

> I grant I am a woman, but withal

In other words, the element of contradiction is introduced with the clause beginning with "but withal". This antithesis becomes even more emphatic through repetition.

As epigrams and antitheses give a pointed quality, so hyperboles give expansion to poetry. There is not much use of hyperbole in this scene, but there is a particularly effective one in Brutus's speech to the conspirators:

> When every drop of blood
> That every Roman bears, and nobly bears,
> Is guilty of a several bastardy.[19]

This hyperbolical statement serves to emphasize the content of Brutus's speech. Later in another passage, Brutus has combined a simile with a hyperbole:

> As dear to me as are the ruddy drops
> That visit my sad heart.[20]

This passage uses not only simile ("as dear to me", etc.) and hyperbole, but also synecdoche, because drops are part of the blood-stream and therefore Brutus has substituted a part for the whole.

These are the most important figures of speech used in this scene. There are several other minor ones as well. There is one figure of speech, however, which has not been used in this scene, but it is so important that it should be mentioned—the masterly use of irony in Antony's Forum speech:

(For Brutus is an honourable man,
So are they all, all honourable men)
. . .   . . .
Yet Brutus say he was ambitious,
And Brutus is an honourable man.
. . .   . . .
Yet Brutus says he was ambitious,
And sure he is an honourable man.[21]

These examples of irony have become the stock examples of this figure of speech in textbooks of rhetoric. Indeed, the entire Forum speech of Antony (as well as that of Brutus) will be very rewarding from this point of view.

Allusion is an important stylistic device. It can be of many types: classical, Biblical, topical, etc. This particular scene does not contain many such, but there is a classical allusion in Brutus's last soliloquy:

Not Erebus itself were dim enough
To hide thee from prevention.[22]

Erebus is a part of the Greek underworld and the allusion is especially apt as Brutus is referring to the dark and evil spirit of conspiracy. There are several such classical allusions elsewhere in the play, as indeed there should be, for the play deals with classical Rome. It is, likewise, not to be wondered at that Biblical allusions, usually plentiful, are few and far between.

One kind of allusion is reference to literary works. Now, in this play there is only one famous literary allusion:

Caesar: *Et tu, Brute*?—Then fall Caesar.[23]

These words, presented as the last words spoken by Caesar, are not given by Plutarch, but by Suetonius.

> Although some have written, that as M.
> Brutus came running upon him he said...
> "And thou my sonne."[24]

This cannot really be called an allusion as such, for they are given as the last words. All the same, they are in Suetonius.

Shakespeare's poetry is usually full of Biblical allusions, which is not the case here. This lack of such references is significant because it points to his consciousness of the fittingness of things. The play is set in pre-Christian times, therefore Biblical allusions would be out of place in it.

Apart from these, there are many other such rhetorical devices scattered throughout the play. Only a few have been cited here and those mainly from one scene. It can be well imagined how rich the entire play is, if judged from this point of view only.

(b) Versification

It has already been pointed out that poetic style can be divided into two categories: the diction and the versification. No discussion of style therefore is complete without a study of the technique of versification. This is not, however, a purely technical aspect of poetry, for it affects the emotional response of the reader and the audience. As Henri Fluchere says:

> It is by its rhythm as much as by its images that a verse is expressive. The rhythmical succession has an emotional pattern, shows a purpose imposing a mood or defining a thought.[25]

The staple poetic form of Elizabethan drama was blank verse, though couplets also were used quite often. Blank verse is a passage of unrhyming lines of five iambic feet. This is a metre in which each foot comprises two syllables, the first weak (or unstressed, or short) and the second is strong (or stressed, or long), as for example:

> Whĕretó / thĕ climb / eř - úp/wărd túrns / hĭs faće;
> Bŭt whén/ hĕ ońce / ăttaińs/thĕ úp/mŏst roúnd,
> Hĕ thén / ŭntó / thĕ ládd / eř twíns / hĭs báck,
> Lŏoks iń / thĕ clóuds /scŏrnińg /thĕ báse / dĕg rées.[26]

This passage has four lines, not rhyming in any way. All the feet are iambic ones. Each line has exactly ten syllables, i.e. five feet. In other words, it is a passage of entirely regular blank verse. It is difficult to find such absolutely regular passages of blank verse, for usually there are many kinds of variations introduced by the poet in order to avoid monotony of rhythm.

These variations in blank verse have many complex features, some of which shall be studied now. One of them is the use of end-stopped and run-on lines. In the passage given above, the first line has a semi-colon at the end so that the actor will have to pause there for a little time. Such a line is an end-stopped line. On the other hand, the lines run on to the next in the passage below:

> Yes, every man of them; and no man here
> But honours you; and every one doth wish
> You had but that opinion of yourself
> Which every noble Roman bears of you.[27]

Here, the actor will not stop at the end of the line, but will go on delivering the next without any break, making an emphatic pause at the end of the fourth line. These are called run-on lines. These and other devices help the poet in avoiding monotony in the poetic delivery. Run-on lines make for a smooth flow and end-stopped lines give a jerky movement. A happy mixture of both create verse with a natural speech rhythm, which is necessary in drama.

It should be remembered that it is not always necessary to avoid end-stopped lines. A poet, especially if he is Shakespeare, can make use of end-stopped lines in order to enhance the naturalness and the beauty of his verse. There is an entire passage of them in the next scene:

> A lioness hath whelped in the streets,
> And graves have yawn'd and yielded up their dead;
> Fierce fiery warriors fight upon the clouds,
> In ranks and squadrons and right form of war,
> Which drizzled blood upon the Capitol.[28]

Here, every line gets emphasis and comes across as strongly as a hammer-blow, for each has a definite pause at the end. Had the lines been run-on ones, the list of supernatural omens given by Calpurnia would not have so effective.

Blank verse lines usually have a brief pause within them known as the caesura, or the medial pause. The placing of the pause in the line is an important factor in versification, for the flexibility of the passage will depend, to a large extent, on this feature. The caesura used to be placed in the middle of the line in mediaeval verse, which used to make the entire poem rather stilted and artificial in movement. This should at all costs, be avoided in drama, unless the writer produces some special effect in a set speech. The Elizabethan dramatist, taking the actor's convenience into account, placed the caesura anywhere within the line in such a way as to facilitate recitation:

> No, my Brutus;
> You have some sick offence // within your mind,
> Which, // by the right and virtue of my place,
> I ought to know of; // and, upon my knees
> I charm you, // by my once commended beauty
> By all your vows of love, // and that great vow.[29]

The double vertical lines indicate the caesura. The positioning of the caesura, counting the syllables comes thus:

Line 2—after the sixth syllable

Line 3—after the first syllable

Line 4—after the fifth syllable

Line 5—after the third syllable

Line 6—after the sixth syllable

This variation makes for great flexibility. Sometimes, there are two or even more, caesurae in a line. Thus Brutus asks:

> Is not to-morrow // boy // the ides of March?[30]

Here, the pauses before and after "boy", is fully justified, as it is a question asked to Lucius. Sometimes, however, multiple caesurae are used for other effects:

> Which, hatch'd, // would, // as his kind, // grow mischievous.[31]

Here, as Brutus is emphasizing a certain point, he pauses after nearly every word and that gives the contemplative quality of the passage great effectiveness.

The definition of Blank Verse is that, it consists of ten syllables to a line. This however, is not an inflexible rule. A line may often have more than ten syllables in it. The line below, for example, has eleven:

> What you/ have said/ and shów/ yourselves/ true Ró/mans.[32]

Sometimes, Shakespeare writes even longer lines, containing twelve syllables, that is, an Alexandrine:

> And these/ does she/ apply/ for warn/ings and portents.[33]

These two are lines slighty longer than a pentameter. Like wise, there might be lines shorter than one. Short lines can be used very effectively:

> Since Cassius first did whet me against Caesar,
> I have not slept.
> Between the acting of a dreadful thing.[34]

The first line of this passage gives the reason for his lack of sleep. Then comes the second line, of only two feet, four syllables. After that, there is a long pause. This heralds in the famous passage beginning with the third line. The mood of contemplation is ushered in with the short line inducing a long pause. There are many short lines in the play, but none is more effective than this.

As this brief discussion shows, really good dramatic blank verse can never be absolutely regular iambic pentameter. There are many other metrical devices that lend the flexibility of speech rhythm to dramatic blank verse. One of them will be mentioned now.

It is dialogue that makes a play what it is, and very often a line is broken up between two or more speakers to avoid monotony. This technique, known as stichomythia, is used quite often by our poet; as given below:

> Cassius: This is Trebonius.
> Brutus: He is welcome hither.

Cas.: This, Decius Brutus.

Bru.: He is welcome too.[35]

Here, a line is broken into two halves by two different speakers. Sometimes, it is broken up into more parts:

Cassius: Who's there?

Casca: A Roman.

Cassius Casca, by your voice.[36]

Here, the one and the same line has been broken up into three parts. The line is to be counted as one. Sometimes, two or more speakers speak in quick succession, capping each other's lines. This device is more popular in comedy.

Brutus: O what a time have you chose out, brave Caius,
To wear a kerchief! Would you were not sick!

Caius: I am not sick if Brutus have in hand
Any exploit worthy the name of honour.

Bru.: Such an exploit have I in hand, Ligarius,
Had you a healthful ear to hear of it.

Cai.: By all the gods that Romans bow before,
I here discard my sickness.[37]

Even though the staple metre of the play is blank verse, couplets are used quite often by Elizabethan dramatists. Sometimes, quite long passages of couplets are put in between blank verse passages. The most popular use of couplets occurs at ends of scenes or Acts. Usually, such couplets serve to sum up the theme of the Act or the scene and often give the emotional attitude of the character. Such couplets are known as Senecan "sentences" because Seneca used such couplets to point out moral lessons. In *Julius Caesar*, there are no passages in couplets, and they occur but rarely at the end of scenes or Acts. As a matter of fact, there are less than ten couplets in the play, and none in this scene. A few examples can be taken. Premonition of the future is given in the first couplet in the play, delivered by Cassius.

And after this, let Caesar seat him sure,
For we will shake him, or worse days endure.[38]

This couplet does not point out a moral. Instead it more or less sums up the conclusion reached by Cassius after his conversation with Brutus and Casca. What is more, it gives premonitions of their future course of action. Very much the same work is done by Artemidorus's couplet at the end of Act II, sc. iii.

Out of the eight couplets in the play, six are to be found in the last Act. Here also there is the unique example of a couplet being broken up between two persons:

Titinius: The sun of Rome is set. Our day is gone
Clouds, dews and dangers come; our deeds are done.
Mistrust of my success hath done this deed.
Mess.: Mistrust of good success hath done this deed.[39]

The second of the couplets has two extraordinary features. First of all, it is divided between two speakers, each speaking a line and secondly it is a tautologous couplet in which except for one word in each line, the same words are used.

Poetic style, in its many different aspects, is but one of the facets of a play, though a very important one. In this chapter the examples, except for certain cases, have been taken from one scene. The earnest reader will realize what enormous variety of imagery and rhetorical figures is scattered throughout the play. Even a limited study like the present one affords a glimpse into the richness and complexity of Shakespeare's poetic style.

NOTES

1. T.S. Dorsch, ed. & transl., *Classical Literary Criticism*, Penguin Books, 1975, p. 83.
2. M.C. Bradbrook, *op. cit.*, p. 45.
3. H. Fluchere, *op. cit.*, p. 152.
4. Quoted in *ibid.*, p. 159.
5. Traversi, *op. cit.*, p. 10.
6. T.S. Dorsch, *op. cit.*, p. 39.
7. Emma Smith, *op. cit.*, p. 7.

8. Act II, sc. i, ll. 32-34, p. 35.
9. Act II, sc. i, ll. 63-65, p. 37.
10. Traversi, *op. cit.*, p. 10.
11. Act II, sc. i, ll. 16-17, p. 34.
12. Act II, sc. i, ll. 22-25, pp. 34-35.
13. Act II, sc. i, ll. 56-58, p. 36.
14. Act II, sc. i, ll. 77-81, p. 38.
15. Act II, sc. i, ll. 123-28, pp. 40-41.
16. Act II, sc. i, l. 14, p. 34.
17. Traversi, *op. cit.*, p. 35.
18. Act II, sc. i, ll. 292-95, p. 48.
19. Act II, sc. i, ll. 136-38, p. 41.
20. Act II, sc. i, ll. 289-90, p. 48.
21. Act III, sc. ii, ll. 84-85, 95-96, 100-01, p. 81.
22. Act II, sc. i, ll. 84-85, p. 39.
23. Act III, sc. i, l. 77, p. 67.
24. Bullough, *op. cit.*, p. 154. The words omitted are in Greek, in Roman Letters they would be, "kai su, teknon".
25. Fluchere, *op. cit.*, p. 181.
26. Act II, sc. i, ll. 23-25, p. 35.
27. Act II, sc. i, ll. 90-93, p. 39.
28. Act II, sc. ii, ll. 17-21, pp. 51-52.
29. Act II, sc. i, ll. 267-72, p. 47.
30. Act II, sc. i, l. 40, p. 35.
31. Act II, sc. i, l. 33, p. 35.
32. Act II, sc. i, l. 223, p. 45.
33. Act II, sc. ii, l. 80, p. 55.
34. Act II, sc. i, ll. 61-63, p. 37.
35. Act II, sc. i, ll. 94-95, p. 39.
36. Act I, sc. iii, l. 41, p. 26.
37. Act II, sc. i, ll. 315-21, p. 49.
38. Act I, sc. ii, ll. 318-19, p. 24.
39. Act V, sc. iii, ll. 63-66, p. 122.

11

Critical Reception: A Brief History

Julius Caesar became an instant success with its very first performance on the stage in 1599. Its popularity has not waned after that. It has been highly popular on the stage as well as in the classrooms, particularly in schools. There is hardly a school in England which has not performed *Julius Caesar*. Both its subject as well as its cast (nearly all-male, with two minor female roles who appear but briefly) has ensured its popularity in boy's schools.

The earliest account of its performance is given by a Swiss traveler Thomas Platter who had been in England from 18th Sept. 1599 to 20th October. He had seen two plays during this time and was highly impressed by this play:

> After lunch on Sept. 21st..., we saw an excellent performance of the tragedy of the first Emperor Julius Caesar with about fifteen characters.[1]

Besides this, there is a reference to the Forum scene in another contemporary work, *The Mirror of Martyrs or the Life and Death of Sir John Oldcastle* by John Weever:

> The many-headed multitude were drawne,
> By Brutus's speech, that Caesar was ambitious,
> When eloquent Mark Antonie had showne
> His vertues, who but Brutus then was vicious?[2]

The play was part of the permanent repertoire of the company and was performed at Court again and again, even forty years later. It continued to be produced on stage during the next two centuries and at the end of the nineteenth century there was an elaborate performance put up by Sir Beerbohm Tree.

It has been equally popular on the screen. An American version was made in which Sir John Gielgud enacted the role of Cassius. There have also been three operas on the play. It was one of the plays produced by Goethe when he was the theatre director at Weimar. Orson Welles had produced an anti-fascist version of the play in modern dress in the early years of the twentieth century.

Later in the century, Triple Action Theatre produced *Julius Caesar* in 1971. It had a cast of only five characters. Its most remarkable feature was its use of a novel technique. Each scene was presented at first like a colourful Roman wall-painting. Then Casca, who was played by a female actress brings the painting to life with his/her clown-like actions. The murder of Caesar was also presented in a novel and innovative manner—a manner which took away all shreds of dignity from the characters:

> Casca strikes Caesar. Caesar runs screaming around the spectators. Cassius and Casca run after him, beating him with their fists and shouting taunts. Caesar runs for protection to Brutus, who strikes him.[3]

Such a presentation might have the virtue of novelty, but how far it is true to Shakespeare is doubtful. It has already been pointed out (*vide* Ch. 9, the section on sources) that Shakespeare presented Julius Caesar in a much more liberal and lenient spirit than Plutarch had. Such a performance presents a degraded view, which the author himself does not.

As far as literary criticism goes, there has not been much critical work on this play, before the middle of the nineteenth century. Ben Jonson had mentioned it in passing and Dryden had briefly discussed the quarrelling scene. Rymer the neo-classicist had criticized all of Shakespeare's plays very severely and *Julius Caesar* did not escape his strictures. According to him Shakespeare's portrayal of the characters had destroyed their nobility. He objects particularly to the blood-bath scene.

Dr. Johnson, too, does not look favourably upon the play. He stigmatizes it as "somewhat cold and unaffecting".

It is noticeable that the first few commentators had been struck by the quarrelling scene between Brutus and Cassius. Colley Cibber had commented upon the stage representation of the scene, in which Betterton had enacted the role of Brutus:

> Thus, with a settled Dignity of Contempt like an unheeding Rock he repelled upon himself the foam of Cassius.[4]

Here, there is dignity and nobility. Voltaire, however, took an extremely derogatory view. He took the play to be a typical example of Anglo-saxon brutality and absurdity:

> These are no Romans who are talking; they are peasants of a past age conspiring in a wine-shop; and Caesar, who invites them to drink a bottle with him, does not in the least resemble Julius Caesar.[5]

With the advent of Romanticism, criticism itself and the attitude of the critics underwent a radical change. The motivation underlying the action of the characters, their psychological make-up, came into focus. Coleridge had pointed out a puzzling feature of Brutus's soliloquy—its ambivalence, but had not given a systematic analysis of the play. Hazlitt, in his study of the characters, points out that the failure of the conspirator's enterprise is to be ascribed to Brutus, though, of course, he does not interpret the character in a negative manner:

> The whole design to liberate their country fails from the generous temper of Brutus, and in his overweening confidence in the goodness of their cause and the assistance of others.[6]

The nineteenth century critics, besides paying more attention to the psychological aspect, also undertook a more systematic study of Shakespeare's plays, covering their different aspects, than had been done heretofore. This came about in the last few decades. It was Paul stapfer who in 1880 suggested a unifying theme in the play and R.G. Moulton analysed the plot in 1885.

In the twentieth century, criticism proliferated and branched out in all directions. No aspect of the play was neglected. A study of the sources was undertaken by G. Bullough whose *Narrative and Dramatic Sources of Shakespeare* still remains the most authoritative book on this subject. A.C. Bradley was definitely the most influential critic of the early twentieth century, and though he has not written on *Julius Caesar* yet his incidental remarks are enlightening and have been referred to in relevant places. Imagery has been studied by Caroline Spurgeon and Wolfgang Clemen. Individual characters have been studied separately. The philosophical background of the play has been studied and so have the stage conventions.

Many critical schools sprang up as the century progressed, like the Marxist school, Feminism, structuralism and many others. These schools, each having its own theory, offer interesting interpretations of Shakespeare's plays. Each such new interpretation reveals different aspects of Shakespeare's plays and their complex, everlasting appeal becomes more and more emphasized.

NOTES

1. Ure, *op. cit.*, p. 27.
2. Dorsch, *op. cit.*, p. vii.
3. Ruby Cohn, *Modern Shakespearean Offshoots*, New Jersey, Princeton Univ. Press, 1976, p. 314.
4. Ure, *op. cit.*, p. 30.
5. *Ibid.*, p. 16.
6. *Ibid.*, p. 32.

Some Important Questions

1. "Here, befitting an historical theme, he returned to a modified form of the chronicle history". Elucidate this remark of Schelling with special reference to *Julius Caesar*.
2. "*Julius Caesar*, the most splendidly written political melodrama we possess". Justify.
3. "It is the spirit of Caesarism that fills the play." Do you agree? Give reasons for your answer.
4. "The action of Julius Caesar turns on a political murder". Analyze the plot in the light of this remark.
5. "Brutus is an intellectual who can do things, who is not hampered by doubts". Analyze the character of Brutus in the light of this remark.
6. "Mark Antony—brilliant, sensuous, devoted to Caesar, but otherwise heartless and treacherous". Sketch the character of Antony in the light of this remark.
7. "The real man Caesar disappears for himself under the greatness of the Caesar myth". Do you agree? Give reasons for your answer.
8. "Cassius was better cut out for a conspirator. His heart prompted his head". Analyze the character of Cassius in the light of this remark.
9. Write a note on the imagery of *Julius Caesar*.
10. What proof of Shakespeare's artistry do you get from the manner in which he used his sources?
11. Give a character sketch of Portia.
12. Write a note on the symbolic importance of the blood-bath in *Julius Caesar*.

Select Bibliography

Bayley, John, *Shakespeare and Tragedy*, Routledge and Kegan Paul, London: 1981.

Bradbrook, M.C., *Themes and Conventions of Elizabethan Tragedy*, Cambridge Univ. Press, 1935.

Bradley, A.C., *Shakespearean Tragedy*, London: Macmillan, 1960.

Clemen, W., *The Development of Shakespeare's Imagery*, London: Methuen, 1951.

Knight, G. Wilson, *The Wheel of Fire*, Oxford: Oxford Univ. Press, 1938.

Leech, Clifford, *Shakespeare's Tragedies*, London: Chatto Windus, 1950.

Ribner, I., *Patterns in Shakespearean Tragedy*, London: Methuen, 1972.

Spencer, T., *Shakespeare and the Nature of Man*, New York: Macmillan, 1945.

Spurgeon, C., *Shakespeare's Imagery and What it Tells Us*, Cambridge University Press, 1935.

Traversi, Derek, *Shakespeare: The Roman Plays*, London: Hollis & Carter, 1963.

Ure, Peter, ed., *Julius Caesar: A Casebook*. London: Macmillan, 1969.

The text used

Dorsch, T.S., ed., *Julius Caesar*, The Arden Shakespeare, New Delhi: B.I. Pubs., 1981 rpt.

Index